Persistence in PHP with Doctrine ORM

Build a model layer of your PHP applications successfully, using Doctrine ORM

Kévin Dunglas

[PACKT] open source✳
PUBLISHING   community experience distilled

BIRMINGHAM - MUMBAI

Persistence in PHP with Doctrine ORM

Copyright © 2013 Packt Publishing

First published: December 2013

Production Reference: 1111213

Published by Packt Publishing Ltd.
Livery Place
35 Livery Street
Birmingham B3 2PB, UK.

ISBN 978-1-78216-410-4

www.packtpub.com

Cover Image by Gagandeep Sharma (er.gagansharma@gmail.com)

Credits

Author
Kévin Dunglas

Reviewers
Kirill Chebunin
Stefan Kleff
Adam Prager
Chris Woodford

Acquisition Editor
Harsha Bharwani

Lead Technical Editor
Vaibhav Pawar

Technical Editors
Nadeem N. Bagban
Venu Manthena
Sebastian Rodrigues

Copy Editors
Alisha Aranha
Sarang Chari
Deepa Nambiar
Gladson Monteiro
Shambhavi Pai
Kirti Pai

Project Coordinator
Ankita Goenka

Proofreader
Bernadette Watkins

Indexer
Tejal Daruwale

Graphics
Sheetal Aute
Abhinash Sahu

Production Coordinator
Arvindkumar Gupta

Cover Work
Arvindkumar Gupta

About the Author

Kévin Dunglas is the co-founder and CEO of La Coopérative des Tilleuls, a French IT company specializing in e-commerce, owned and managed by its workers themselves. He is also a software architect who works for a lot of companies, including Ubisoft and SensioLabs (creator of Symfony), as an external contractor. He contributes to open source software (especially Symfony, JavaScript, and Ubuntu ecosystems) and has been writing a technical blog for more than 10 years.

About the Reviewers

Kirill Chebunin is a software engineer specializing in server-side web development. His main interests lie in the field of systems with complex background logic. He has been working as the head of a PHP development department, building different enterprises, and billing and analytics systems for the last two years. But his real passion is for open source projects and their communities. Kirill's talks can be found in Russian and Ukrainian PHP conferences, and his commits are presented in Composer, Doctrine, and Symfony projects. You can always see his current interests at Github (`https://github.com/chebba`) and SlideShare (`http://www.slideshare.net/chebba`).

Stefan Kleff has been developing web applications for over 12 years at various positions in various companies. He holds degrees from the University of Applied Sciences in Iserlohn, as well as the Hasso Plattner Institute of Computer Science. In a cooperation class with Stanford University, he acquired practical knowledge of Design Thinking. Stefan is an active contributor to the Doctrine project and Zend Framework 2. Currently, he is working as a Project Manager at webXells GmbH and is the co-founder of goalio UG in Potsdam, Germany.

Adam Prager is a full stack web application developer who has created many data-heavy business management applications in the areas of Customer Relationship Management (CRM), Enterprise Resource Planning (ERP), and Laboratory Information Management System (LIMS). He is a big believer in the value and power of open source software, and contributes to projects such as Doctrine and Symfony regularly on Github. He has published numerous Symfony bundles and jQuery plugins of his own. Adam currently works for Netlife in Hungary. Netlife is a Consulting and IT services company, which provides web application development services using the latest technologies, and complete business solutions based on SAP consulting. As a diverse end-to-end IT solutions provider, Netlife offers a range of expertise aimed at assisting customers to compete successfully in the ever changing IT industry. They provide long term solutions with a focus on quality. They have excellent domain expertise in SAP, CRM, custom web application development, and user experience design.

Chris Woodford is a web software consultant and entrepreneur based in Toronto, Canada. He has been working with modern web technologies (Ruby, nodeJS, and PHP) for over 10 years, with a focus on solving tough problems. In his spare time, he co-runs a small record label, Hypaethral Records (`http://hypaethralrecords.com`) and tours the world with his band TITAN (`http://titanslays.com`).

www.PacktPub.com

Support files, eBooks, discount offers and more

You might want to visit www.PacktPub.com for support files and downloads related to your book.

Did you know that Packt offers eBook versions of every book published, with PDF and ePub files available? You can upgrade to the eBook version at www.PacktPub.com and as a print book customer, you are entitled to a discount on the eBook copy. Get in touch with us at service@packtpub.com for more details.

At www.PacktPub.com, you can also read a collection of free technical articles, sign up for a range of free newsletters and receive exclusive discounts and offers on Packt books and eBooks.

http://PacktLib.PacktPub.com

Do you need instant solutions to your IT questions? PacktLib is Packt's online digital book library. Here, you can access, read and search across Packt's entire library of books.

Why Subscribe?

- Fully searchable across every book published by Packt
- Copy and paste, print and bookmark content
- On demand and accessible via web browser

Free Access for Packt account holders

If you have an account with Packt at www.PacktPub.com, you can use this to access PacktLib today and view nine entirely free books. Simply use your login credentials for immediate access.

Table of Contents

Preface   **1**

Chapter 1: Getting Started with Doctrine 2   **5**

   Prerequisites   **7**

   Understanding the concepts behind Doctrine   **8**

   Creating a project structure   **10**

   Installing Composer   **11**

   Installing Doctrine   **11**

   Bootstrapping the app   **13**

   Using Doctrine's Entity Manager   **14**

   Configuring Doctrine command-line tools   **16**

   Summary   **17**

Chapter 2: Entities and Mapping Information   **19**

   Creating the Entity class   **20**

   Generating getters and setters   **21**

   Mapping with Doctrine annotations   **22**

      Knowing about the @Entity annotation   22

      Understanding the @Table, @Index, and

      @UniqueConstraint annotations   22

      Diving into the @Column annotation   23

      Knowing about the @Id and @GeneratedValue annotations   24

      Using other annotations   25

   Understanding Doctrine Mapping Types   **25**

   Creating the database schema   **26**

   Installing Data fixtures   **28**

   Creating a simple UI   **30**

      Listing posts   31

      Creating and editing posts   33

Deleting posts	37
Summary	**38**
Chapter 3: Associations	**39**
Getting started with the Doctrine associations	**39**
Understanding the @ManyToOne and @OneToMany annotations with the comment system	**40**
Creating the Comment entity class (owning side)	41
Adding the inverse side to the Post entity class	43
Updating the database schema	45
Adding fixtures for the comments	46
Listing and creating comments	47
Updating the index	51
Understanding the @ManyToMany annotation with tags	**52**
Creating the Tag entity class (inverse side)	52
Updating the Post entity class (owning side)	54
Updating the schema again	56
Creating tag fixtures	56
Managing the tags of a post	58
Summary	**59**
Chapter 4: Building Queries	**61**
Understanding DQL	**61**
Using the entity repositories	**63**
Creating custom entity repositories	64
Getting started with Query Builder	**65**
Filtering by tag	**69**
Counting comments	**71**
Summary	**73**
Chapter 5: Going Further	**75**
Implementing inheritance	**75**
Using Mapped Superclasses	76
Using Single Table Inheritance	82
Using Class Table Inheritance	84
Getting started with events	**86**
Lifecycle callbacks	87
Knowing about event listeners and event subscribers	89
Writing native queries	**92**
The NativeQuery class	92
Doctrine DBAL	94
Summary	**96**
Index	**97**

Preface

Doctrine 2 has become the most popular modern persistence system for PHP. It is distributed with the standard edition of the Symfony2 framework, can be used standalone in any PHP project and integrates very well with Zend Framework 2, CodeIgniter, or Laravel. It is efficient, automatically abstracts popular database managing systems, supports PHP 5.3 features (including namespaces), is installable through Composer, and has an extensively tested quality code base.

Doctrine's ORM library allows easy persisting and retrieving of PHP object graph, without writing any SQL query by hand. It also provides a powerful object-oriented SQL-like query language called DQL, a database schema generator tool, an event system, and much more.

To discover this must-have library, we will together build a typical small, blog engine.

What this book covers

Chapter 1, Getting Started with Doctrine 2, explains how to install Common, DBAL, and ORM libraries through Composer, get our first entity manager, and configure command-line tools after presenting the project we built throughout the book (the architecture of Doctrine and the configuration of the development environment).

Chapter 2, Entities and Mapping Information, introduces the concept of Doctrine entities. We will create a first entity, map it to the database with annotations, generate the database schema, create data fixtures, and, finally, lay the foundation of the user interface of the blog.

Chapter 3, Associations, explains how to handle associations between the PHP objects and the ORM. We will create new entities, detail one-to-one, one-to-many, and many-to-many associations, generate the underlying database schema, create data fixtures and use associations in the user interface.

Chapter 4, Building Queries, creates entity repositories and helps understand how to use the query builder for generating DQL queries and retrieving entities. We will also take a look at aggregate functions.

Chapter 5, Going Further, will take a look at the advanced features of Doctrine. We will see different ways in which Doctrine can manage object inheritance, play with entity lifecycle events, and create native SQL queries.

What you need for this book

To execute examples of this book, you just need PHP 5.4+ a text editor, or a PHP IDE, and your favorite browser.

Who this book is for

Readers should have a good knowledge of object-oriented programming, PHP (including features introduced in PHP 5.3 and 5.4), and general database concepts.

Conventions

In this book, you will find a number of styles of text that distinguish between different kinds of information. Here are some examples of these styles, and an explanation of their meaning.

Code words in text, database table names, folder names, filenames, file extensions, pathnames, dummy URLs, and user input are shown as follows: "The NativeQuery class allows you to execute native SQL queries and to get their results as Doctrine entities."

A block of code is set as follows:

```
/**
 * Adds comment
 *
 * @param  Comment $comment
 * @return Post
 */
public function addComment(Comment $comment)
{
    $this->comments[] = $comment;
    $comment->setPost($this);

    return $this;
}
```

When we wish to draw your attention to a particular part of a code block, the relevant lines or items are set in bold:

```
/**
 * Adds comment
 *
 * @param  Comment $comment
 * @return Post
 */
public function addComment(Comment $comment)
{
    $this->comments[] = $comment;
    $comment->setPost($this);

    return $this;
}
```

Any command-line input or output is written as follows:

```
# php bin/load-fixtures.php
```

New terms and **important words** are shown in bold. Words that you see on the screen, in menus or dialog boxes for example, appear in the text like this: "The following text must be printed in the terminal: **ATTENTION: This operation should not be executed in a production environment**."

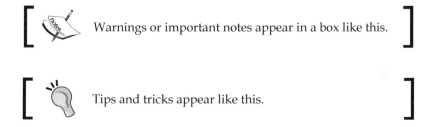

Warnings or important notes appear in a box like this.

Tips and tricks appear like this.

Reader feedback

Feedback from our readers is always welcome. Let us know what you think about this book—what you liked or may have disliked. Reader feedback is important for us to develop titles that you really get the most out of.

To send us general feedback, simply send an e-mail to feedback@packtpub.com, and mention the book title via the subject of your message.

If there is a topic that you have expertise in and you are interested in either writing or contributing to a book, see our author guide on www.packtpub.com/authors.

Customer support

Now that you are the proud owner of a Packt book, we have a number of things to help you to get the most from your purchase.

Downloading the example code

You can download the example code files for all Packt books you have purchased from your account at `http://www.packtpub.com`. If you purchased this book elsewhere, you can visit `http://www.packtpub.com/support` and register to have the files e-mailed directly to you.

Errata

Although we have taken every care to ensure the accuracy of our content, mistakes do happen. If you find a mistake in one of our books—maybe a mistake in the text or the code—we would be grateful if you would report this to us. By doing so, you can save other readers from frustration and help us improve subsequent versions of this book. If you find any errata, please report them by visiting `http://www.packtpub.com/submit-errata`, selecting your book, clicking on the **errata submission form** link, and entering the details of your errata. Once your errata are verified, your submission will be accepted and the errata will be uploaded on our website, or added to any list of existing errata, under the Errata section of that title. Any existing errata can be viewed by selecting your title from `http://www.packtpub.com/support`.

Piracy

Piracy of copyright material on the Internet is an ongoing problem across all media. At Packt, we take the protection of our copyright and licenses very seriously. If you come across any illegal copies of our works, in any form, on the Internet, please provide us with the location address or website name immediately so that we can pursue a remedy.

Please contact us at `copyright@packtpub.com` with a link to the suspected pirated material.

We appreciate your help in protecting our authors, and our ability to bring you valuable content.

Questions

You can contact us at `questions@packtpub.com` if you are having a problem with any aspect of the book, and we will do our best to address it.

1
Getting Started with Doctrine 2

The Doctrine project is a collection of libraries providing utilities to ease data persistence in PHP applications. It makes it possible to create complex model layers in no time that will be compatible with popular DBMS, including SQLite, MySQL, and PostgreSQL. To discover and understand Doctrine, we will create a small blog from scratch throughout this book that will mainly use the following Doctrine components:

- **Common** provides utilities that are not in the PHP standard library including a class autoloader, an annotations parser, collections structures, and a cache system.

- **Database Abstraction Layer (DBAL)** exposes a unique interface to access popular DBMS. Its API is similar to PDO (and PDO is used when possible). The DBAL component is also able to execute the same SQL query on different DBMS by internally rewriting the query to use specific constructs and emulate missing features.

- **Object Relational Mapper (ORM)** allows accessing and managing relational database tables and rows through an object-oriented API. Thanks to it, we will directly manipulate PHP objects, and it will transparently generate SQL queries to populate, persist, update, and delete them. It is built on top of DBAL and will be the main topic of this book.

 For more information on PHP Data Objects and the data-access abstraction layer provided by PHP, refer to the following link:
`http://php.net/manual/en/book.pdo.php`

To learn Doctrine, we will build together a tiny blog engine with advanced features such as the following:

- Posts list, creation, editing, and deletion
- Comments
- Tag filtering
- Profiles for author of posts and comments
- Statistics
- Data fixtures

The following is a screenshot of the blog:

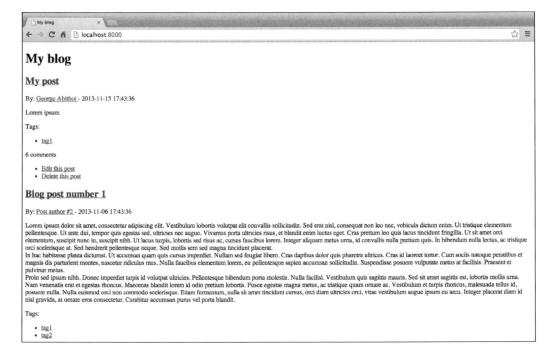

In this chapter, we will learn about the following topics:

- Understanding concepts behind Doctrine
- Creating the project's structure
- Installing Composer
- Installing Doctrine ORM, DBAL, and Common through Compose
- Bootstrapping the app
- Using Doctrine's Entity Manager
- Configuring Doctrine command-line tools

Prerequisites

To follow this tutorial, we need a proper CLI installation of PHP 5.4 or superior. We will also use the `curl` command to download the Composer archive and the SQLite 3 client.

> For further information about PHP CLI, curl, and SQLite, refer to the following links: `http://www.php.net/manual/en/features.commandline.php`, `http://curl.haxx.se`, and `http://www.sqlite.org`

In the examples, we will use the PHP built-in web server and SQLite as DBMS. Doctrine is a pure PHP library. It is compatible with any web server supporting PHP, but is not limited to Apache and Nginx. Of course, it can also be used in applications that are not intended to run on web servers, such as command-line tools. On the database side, SQLite, MySQL, PostgreSQL, Oracle, and Microsoft SQL Server are officially supported.

Thanks to the DBAL component, our blog should work fine with all these DBMS. It has been tested with SQLite and MySQL.

The Doctrine project also provides **Object Document Mappers (ODM)** for NoSQL databases including MongoDB, CouchDB, PHPCR, and OrientDB. These topics are not covered in this book.

> Do not hesitate to consult the Doctrine documentation specified in the following link while reading this book: `http://www.doctrine-project.org`

Understanding the concepts behind Doctrine

Doctrine ORM implements **Data Mapper** and **Unit of Work** design patterns.

The Data Mapper is a layer designed to synchronize data stored in database with their related objects of the domain layer. In other words, it does the following:

- Inserts and updates rows in the database from data held by object properties
- Deletes rows in the database when related entities are marked for deletion
- **Hydrates** in-memory objects with data retrieved from the database

For more information about the Data Mapper and Unit of Work design patterns, you can refer to the following links: `http://martinfowler.com/eaaCatalog/dataMapper.html` and `http://martinfowler.com/eaaCatalog/unitOfWork.html`

In the Doctrine terminology, a Data Mapper is called an **Entity Manager**. Entities are plain old PHP objects of the domain layer.

Thanks to the Entity Manager, they don't have to be aware that they will be stored in a database. In fact, they don't need to be aware of the existence of the Entity Manager itself. This design pattern allows reusing entity classes regardless of the persistence system.

For performance and data consistency, the Entity Manager does not sync entities with the database each time they are modified. The Unit of Work design pattern is used to keep the states of objects managed by the Data Mapper. Database synchronization happens only when requested by a call to the `flush()` method of the Entity Manager and is done in a transaction (if something goes wrong while synchronizing entities to the database, the database will be rolled back to its state prior to the synchronization attempt).

Imagine an entity with a public `$name` property. Imagine the following code being executed:

```
$myEntity->name = 'My name';
$myEntity->name = 'Kévin';
$entityManager->flush($myEntity);
```

Thanks to the implementation of the Unit of Work design pattern, only one SQL query similar to the following will be issued by Doctrine:

```
UPDATE MyEntity SET name='Kévin' WHERE id=1312;
```

The query is similar because, for performance reasons, Doctrine uses prepared statements.

We will finish the theory part with a short overview of the Entity Manager methods and their related entity states.

The following is an extract of a class diagram representing an entity and its Entity Manager:

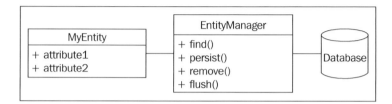

- The `find()` method **hydrates** and returns an entity of the type **passed** in the first parameter having the second parameter as an **identifier**. Data is retrieved from the database through a SELECT query. The state of this returned entity is **managed**. It means that when the `flush()` method is called, changes made to it will be synced to the database. The `find()` method is a convenience method that internally uses an **entity repository** to retrieve data from the database and hydrate the entity. The state of the managed entities can be changed to **detached** by calling the `detach()` method. Modifications made to the detached entity will not be synced to the database (even when the `flush()` method is called) until its state is set back to **managed** with a call to the `merge()` method.

 The start of *Chapter 3, Associations*, will be dedicated to entity repositories.

- The `persist()` method tells Doctrine to set the state of the entity passed in parameter as managed. This is only useful for entities that have not been synced at least one time to the database (the default state of a newly created object is **new**) because entities hydrated from existing data automatically have the managed state.

- The remove() method sets the state of the passed in entity to **removed**. Data related to this entity will be effectively removed from the database with a DELETE SQL query the next time the flush() method is called.

- The flush() method syncs data of entities with **managed** and **removed** states to the database. Doctrine will issue INSERT, UPDATE, and DELETE SQL queries for the sync. Before that call, all changes are only in-memory and are never synchronized to the database.

 Doctrine's Entity Manager has a lot of other useful methods documented on the Doctrine website, http://www.doctrine-project.org/api/orm/2.4/class-Doctrine.ORM.EntityManager.html.

This is abstract for now, but we will understand better how the Entity Manager works with numerous examples throughout the book.

Creating a project structure

The following is the folder structure of our app:

- blog/: App root created earlier
- bin/: Specific command line tools of our blog app
- config/: Configuration files of our app
- data/: The SQLite database will be stored here
- src/: All PHP classes we write will be here
- vendor/: This is where **Composer** (see the following section) stores all downloaded dependencies including the source code of Doctrine
- bin/: This is a command-line tool provided by dependencies installed with Composer
- web/: This is the public directory that contains PHP pages and assets such as images, CSS, and JavaScript files

We must create all these directories except the vendor/ one that will be automatically generated later.

Installing Composer

As with most modern PHP libraries, Doctrine is available through Composer, a powerful dependency manager. A PEAR channel is also available.

 For more information on Composer and Pear packages, please refer to the respective links as follows: `http://getcomposer.org` and `http://pear.doctrine-project.org`

The following steps should be performed to install Composer:

1. The first step to install Doctrine ORM is to grab a copy of the latest Composer version.

2. Open your preferred terminal, go to the `blog/` directory (the root of our project), and type the following command to install Composer:

   ```
   curl -sS https://getcomposer.org/installer | php
   ```

   A new file called `composer.phar` has been downloaded in the directory. This is a self-contained archive of Composer.

3. Now type the following command:

   ```
   php composer.phar
   ```

   If everything is OK, all available commands are listed. Your Composer installation is up and running!

Installing Doctrine

The following steps should be performed to install Doctrine:

1. To install Doctrine, we need to create a file called `composer.json` in our new `blog` directory. It lists dependencies of our project as shown in the following code:

   ```
   {
       "name": "myname/blog",
       "type": "project",
       "description": "My small blog to play with Doctrine",

       "require": {
   ```

```
        "doctrine/orm": "2.4.*"
    },

    "autoload": {
        "psr-0": { "": "src/" }
    }
}
```

This standard JSON file will be parsed by Composer to download and install all dependencies specified. Once installed, Composer will load all classes of these libraries automatically.

The name, type, and description attributes are optional but it's a good practice to always fill them. They provide general information about the project we are working on.

The more interesting part of this composer.json file is the require field. In order to get it installed by Composer, all libraries used by our app must be listed here. A lot of PHP libraries are available on **Packagist**, the default Composer package repository. Of course, it's the case of Doctrine projects.

 For more information on Packagist, go through the following link: https://packagist.org/

We indicate that we need the latest minor release of the 2.4 branch of Doctrine ORM. You can set a major or minor version here, and even more complicated things.

 For more information on a package version, you can refer to the following link: http://getcomposer.org/doc/01-basic-usage.md#package-versions

The autoload field is here to tell Composer to automatically load classes of our app. We will put our specific code in a directory called src/. Our files and classes will follow the PSR-0 namespacing and file-naming standard.

 PHP Specification Requests are attempts to improve interoperability of PHP applications and libraries. They are available at http://www.php-fig.org/.

2. It's time to use Composer to install the ORM. Run the following command:

```
php composer.phar install
```

New files appear in the `vendor/` directory. Doctrine ORM has been installed, and Composer was smart enough to get all its dependencies, including Doctrine DBAL and Doctrine Common.

A `composer.lock` file has also been created. It contains exact versions of installed libraries. This is useful for deploying applications. Thanks to this file, when running the `install` command, Composer will be able to retrieve the same versions that have been used in the development.

Doctrine is now properly installed. Easy, isn't it?

3. To update libraries when there are new releases in the 2.4 branch, we just need to type the following command:

```
php composer.phar update
```

Bootstrapping the app

The following steps need to be performed for bootstrapping the app:

1. Create a new file called `config/config.php` that will contain configuration parameters of our app as shown in the following code:

```php
<?php

// App configuration
$dbParams = [
  'driver' => 'pdo_sqlite',
  'path' => __DIR__.'/../data/blog.db'
];

// Dev mode?
$dev = true;
```

The Doctrine configuration parameters are stored in the `$dbParams` array. We will use a SQLite Database called `blog.db` stored in the `data/` directory. If you want to use MySQL or any other DBMS, it's here that you will configure the driver to use, the database name, and the access credentials.

The following is a sample configuration to use MySQL instead of SQLite:

```
$dbParams = [
    'driver' => 'pdo_mysql',
    'host' => '127.0.0.1',
    'dbname' => 'blog',
    'user' => 'root',
    'password' => ''
];
```

Config keys are self-explanatory.

If the `$dev` variable is `true`, some optimizations will be disabled to ease debugging. Disabling the `dev` mode allows Doctrine to put a lot of data such as metadata in powerful caches to increase overall performances of the app.

It requires cache driver installation and extra configuration, which is available at `http://docs.doctrine-project.org/en/latest/reference/caching.html`.

2. Next, we need a way to bootstrap our app. Create a file called `bootstrap.php` in the `src/` directory. This file will load everything we need as given in the following code:

```
<?php

require_once __DIR__.'/../vendor/autoload.php';
require_once __DIR__.'/../config/config.php';
```

The first line requires the Composer autoloader. It allows you to automatically load the Doctrine's classes, the project's classes (that will be in the `src/` directory), and any class of a library installed with Composer.

The second line imports the configuration file of the app. The project structure is created and the initialization process of the app is done. We are ready to start using Doctrine.

Using Doctrine's Entity Manager

The principle of an ORM is to manage data stored in a relational database through an object-oriented API. We learned about its underlying concepts earlier in this chapter.

Each entity class is mapped to the related database table. Properties of the entity class are mapped to the table's columns.

So, the rows of a database table are represented in the PHP app by a collection of entities.

Doctrine ORM is able to retrieve data from the database and to populate entities with them. This process is called hydration.

 Instead of entities, Doctrine can populate PHP arrays in different manners (with the object graph, with a rectangular result set, and so on). It is also possible to create custom hydrators by referring to the following link: `http://docs.doctrine-project.org/en/latest/reference/dql-doctrine-query-language.html#hydration-modes`

As we have learned with the Data Mapper design pattern, it also does the inverse job: it persists data held by entities to database.

We will play a lot with entities later.

Doctrine comes with the following files to map entities to tables:

- Annotations in comment blocks that embed directly in the entities
- XML configuration files
- YAML configuration files
- Plain PHP files

Annotations are fairly recent in the PHP world (they are popular in Java) but they are already widely used by Doctrine and Symfony communities. The advantages of this method are great readability and maintenance facility because mapping information is next to the PHP code. Putting mapping information directly in the code can also be a drawback in some contexts, especially for big projects that use several persistence systems.

We will use the annotation method in this book, but other methods are described in the Doctrine documentation. We will return to them in *Chapter 2, Entities and Mapping Information*.

In the next chapter, *Chapter 2, Entities and Mapping Information*, we will discover that Doctrine is smart enough to use mapping information to automatically create the related database schema.

For now, we will focus on retrieving an Entity Manager. As entities are retrieved, persisted, updated, and removed through it, this is the entry point of Doctrine ORM.

Edit the `src/bootstrap.php` file to retrieve a Doctrine's Entity Manager. Add the following code at the end of this file:

```
$entitiesPath = array(__DIR__.'/Blog/Entity');
$config = Setup::createAnnotationMetadataConfiguration
  ($entitiesPath, $dev);
$entityManager = EntityManager::create($dbParams, $config);
```

Downloading the example code

You can download the example code files for all Packt books you have purchased from your account at `http://www.packtpub.com`. If you purchased this book elsewhere, you can visit `http://www.packtpub.com/support` and register to have the files e-mailed directly to you.

The `$entitiesPath` property contains the list of paths to directories storing entity classes. We already mentioned that our app will follow the PSR-0 namespacing convention. The `\Blog` folder will be the root namespace and entity classes will be in the `\Blog\Entity` folder.

A Doctrine configuration is created to use annotations for mapping information and to be able to locate the blog's entities that we'll create.

A new `EntityManager` is created and configured to use our database and Doctrine settings.

For simplicity, we create a unique Entity Manager that will be used across the application. For real-world apps, you should take a look at the Dependency Injection design pattern.

Find more on Dependency Injection pattern at the following link:
`http://en.wikipedia.org/wiki/Dependency_injection`

Configuring Doctrine command-line tools

The Doctrine library is bundled with some useful command line tools. They provide many helpful features, including, but not limited to the ability to create database schema from entity mappings.

Composer has installed Doctrine's command line tools in the `vendor/bin/` directory. But before being able to use them, a bit of configuration must be done. Command line tools internally use an Entity Manager. We need to tell them how to retrieve it.

Here, we just need to create one more file called `cli-config.php` in the `config/` directory as follows:

```php
<?php

// Doctrine CLI configuration file

use Doctrine\ORM\Tools\Console\ConsoleRunner;

require_once __DIR__.'/../src/bootstrap.php';

return ConsoleRunner::createHelperSet($entityManager);
```

Thanks to the Doctrine's conventions, the file will be automatically detected and used by the Doctrine CLI.

 Command line tools will look for a file called `cli-config.php` in the current directory and in the `config/` directory.

This file just gets a new Entity Manager using the utility class we've created earlier and configures the Doctrine CLI to use it.

Type the following command to get a list of available Doctrine commands:

```
php vendor/bin/doctrine.php
```

Summary

In this chapter, we discovered the fundamentals of Doctrine. We now know what entities and Entity Managers are, we have installed Doctrine with the Composer dependency manager, we created the skeleton of our blog app, and we managed to get the command line tools up and running.

In the next chapter, we will create our first entity class, discover a lot of annotations to map it to the database, generate the database schema, and start dealing with entities. By the end of the next chapter, the post system of our blog will be working!

2
Entities and Mapping Information

In the previous chapter, we discovered the concepts behind Doctrine, we learned how to use Composer to install it, we set up the Doctrine Command Line Tools and we dived into the Entity Manager.

In this chapter, we will cover the following topics:

- Creating our first entity class
- Mapping it to its related database table and columns with annotations
- Using a command helper provided by Doctrine to automatically generate the database schema
- Creating some fixtures data and dealing with the Entity Manager to display our data in a web user interface

Because we are building a blog, our main entity class will be called Post, as shown in the following figure:

Post
id : int
title : string
body : string
publicationDate : \DateTime

Our `Post` entity class has the following four properties:

- `id`: The unique identifier of the post across the database table (and the blog)
- `title`: The post's title
- `body`: The post's body
- `publicationDate`: The date of publication of the post

Creating the Entity class

As explained in *Chapter 1, Getting Started with Doctrine 2*, a Doctrine entity is just a PHP object that will be saved in the database. Doctrine annotations are added in the PHP `DocBlock` comments of the Entity class properties. Annotations are used by Doctrine to map the object to the related database's table and properties to columns.

 The original purpose of **DocBlocks** is integrating technical documentation directly in the source code. The most popular documentation generator that parses DocBlocks is **phpDocumentator** which is available on this website: `http://www.phpdoc.org`.

Each entity, once persisted through Doctrine, will be related to a row of the database's table.

Create a new file `Post.php` containing our entity class in the `src/Blog/Entity/` location with the following code:

```php
<?php

namespace Blog\Entity;

use Doctrine\ORM\Mapping\Entity;
use Doctrine\ORM\Mapping\Table;
use Doctrine\ORM\Mapping\Index;
use Doctrine\ORM\Mapping\Id;
use Doctrine\ORM\Mapping\GeneratedValue;
use Doctrine\ORM\Mapping\Column;

/**
 * Blog Post entity
 *
 * @Entity
 * @Table(indexes={
```

```
 *          @Index(name="publication_date_idx",
  columns="publicationDate")
 * })
 */
class Post
{
  /**
   * @var int
   *
   * @Id
   * @GeneratedValue
   * @Column(type="integer")
   */
  protected $id;
  /**
   * @var string
   *
   * @Column(type="string")
   */
  protected $title;
  /**
   * @var string
   *
   * @Column(type="text")
   */
  protected $body;
  /**
   * @var \DateTime
   *
   * @Column(type="datetime")
   */
  protected $publicationDate;
}
```

Generating getters and setters

Doctrine command-line tools that we configured in *Chapter 1, Getting Started with Doctrine 2*, include a useful command that generates getter and setter methods of an Entity class for us. We will use it to save us from having to write those of the Post class.

Run the following command to generate getters and setters of all entity classes of the application:

```
php vendor/bin/doctrine.php orm:generate:entities src/
```

If you have several entities and don't want to generate getters and setters for all of them, use the `filter` option with the `orm:generate:entities` command.

Mapping with Doctrine annotations

`Post` is a simple class with four properties. The setter for `$id` isn't actually generated. Doctrine populates the `$id` instance variable directly in the entity hydration phase. We will see later how we delegate the ID generation to the DBMS.

Doctrine annotations are imported from the `\Doctrine\ORM\Mapping` namespace with `use` statements. They are used in DocBlocks to add mapping information to the class and its properties. DocBlocks are just a special kind of comment starting with `/**`.

Knowing about the @Entity annotation

The `@Entity` annotation is used in the class-level DocBlock to specify that this class is an entity class.

The most important attribute of this annotation is `repositoryClass`. It allows specifying a custom entity repository class. We will learn about entity repositories, including how to make a custom one, in *Chapter 4*, *Building Queries*.

Understanding the @Table, @Index, and @UniqueConstraint annotations

The `@Table` annotation is optional. It can be used to add some mapping information to the table related to the entity class.

The related database table name is default to the entity class name. Here, it is `Post`. It can be changed using the `name` attribute of the annotation. This is a good practice to let Doctrine automatically generate the table and column names but it can be useful to change them to match a preexisting schema.

As you can see, we use the `@Table` annotation to create indexes on the underlying table. To do that, we use an attribute called `indexes` that contains a list of indexes. Each index is defined by an `@Index` annotation. Each `@Index` must contain the following two attributes:

- `name`: The name of the index
- `columns`: The list of indexed columns

For the `Post` entity class, we create an index on the `publicationDate` column called `publication_date_idx`.

The last optional attribute of the `@Table` annotation is `uniqueConstraints` (not used here). It allows creating SQL level unique constraints on columns and groups of columns. Its syntax is similar to `@Index`: `name` to name the constraint and `columns` to specify the columns on which it applies the constraints.

This attribute is only used by the schema generator. Even if the `uniqueConstraints` attribute is used, Doctrine will not automatically check that a value is unique across a table. The underlying DBMS will do this, but it can lead to DBMS level SQL errors. If we want to enforce uniqueness of data, we should perform a check prior to saving new data.

Diving into the @Column annotation

Each property is mapped to a database column thanks to the `@Column` annotation.

The name of the mapped database column defaults to the property name but can be changed with the `name` parameter. As for table names, it's better to let Doctrine generate names by itself.

> As in the case of table names, column names will default to entity class property names (Camel case if the PSR style is correctly followed).
>
> Doctrine also comes with an underscore naming strategy (for instance, the database table related to a class called `MyEntity` will be `my_entity`) and it is possible to write custom strategies.
>
> Learn more about this in the Doctrine documentation: `http://docs.doctrine-project.org/en/latest/reference/namingstrategy.html`

If a property is not marked with the `@Column` annotation, Doctrine will ignore it.

Its `type` attribute indicates the Doctrine Mapping Type of the column (see next section). It is the only required attribute of this annotation.

This annotation supports some more attributes. Like for every other annotation, the full list of supported attributes is available in the Doctrine documentation. The most important attributes are as follows:

- `unique`: If `true`, the value of this column must be unique across the related database table

- `nullable`: If `false`, the value can be NULL. By default, columns cannot be NULL.

- `length`: The length of the column for values of the `string` type

- `scale`: The scale for columns for values of the `decimal` type

- `precision`: The precision for columns for values of the `decimal` type

As for `@Table`, Doctrine does not use attributes of the `@Column` annotation to validate data. These attributes are only used for the mapping and to generate the database schema. Nothing more. For security and user experience reasons, you must validate every piece of data provided by users. This book does not cover this topic. If you do not want to handle data validation manually, try the Symfony Validator Component from `http://symfony.com/components/Validator`.

> It's also possible to use lifecycle events (see *Chapter 5, Going Further*) to handle data validation: `http://docs.doctrine-project.org/projects/doctrine-orm/en/latest/cookbook/validation-of-entities.html`

Knowing about the @Id and @GeneratedValue annotations

The `$id` property is a bit special. This is a column mapped to an integer, but this is mainly the unique identifier of our object.

Through the `@Id` annotation, this column will be used as the primary key of the table.

By default, it is the responsibility of the developer to ensure that the value of this property is unique across the table. Almost all DBMSs provide mechanisms to automatically increment an identifier at the insertion of a new row. The `@GeneratedValue` annotation takes advantage of this. When a property is marked with `@GeneratedValue`, Doctrine will delegate the generation of the identifier to the underlying DBMS.

> Other ID generation strategies are available at `http://docs.doctrine-project.org/en/latest/reference/basic-mapping.html#identifier-generation-strategies`.

Doctrine also supports composite primary keys. Just add an `@Id` annotation to all columns of your composite primary key.

We will study another example using a unique string as identifier in *Chapter 3, Associations*.

Using other annotations

A lot of Doctrine mapping annotations exist. We will use some new annotations in *Chapter 3, Associations* to create relations between entities.

The full list of available annotation is given in the Doctrine documentation at `http://docs.doctrine-project.org/projects/doctrine-orm/en/latest/reference/annotations-reference.html`.

Understanding Doctrine Mapping Types

Doctrine Mapping Types used in the `@Column` annotation are neither SQL types nor PHP types but they are mapped to both. For instance, the Doctrine `text` type will be casted to the `string` PHP type in the entity and stored in a database column with the `CLOB` type.

The following is a correspondence table for Doctrine Mapping Type of PHP type and SQL type:

Doctrine Mapping Type	PHP Type	SQL Type
string	string	VARCHAR
integer	integer	INT
smallint	integer	SMALLINT
bigint	string	BIGINT
boolean	boolean	BOOLEAN
decimal	double	DECIMAL
date	\DateTime	DATETIME
time	\DateTime	TIME
datetime	\DateTime	DATETIME or TIMESTAMP
text	string	CLOB
object	object using the serialize() and unserialize() methods	CLOB
array	array using serialize() and unserialize() methods	CLOB
float	double	FLOAT (double precision)
simple_array	array using implode() and explode() Values cannot contain comma.	CLOB

Doctrine Mapping Type	PHP Type	SQL Type
`json_array`	`object` using `json_encode()` and `json_decode()` methods	CLOB
`guid`	`string`	GUID or UUID if supported by the DBMS, VARCHAR either
`blob`	`resource stream` (see `http://www.php.net/manual/en/language.types.resource.php`)	BLOB

 Keep in mind that we can create custom types. To learn more about this, refer to: `http://docs.doctrine-project.org/en/latest/cookbook/custom-mapping-types.html`

Creating the database schema

Doctrine is smart enough to generate the database schema corresponding to the entity mapping information.

 It's a good practice to always design entities first and to generate the related database schema after that.

To do this, we will again use Command-Line Tools installed in the first chapter. Type this command in the root directory of our project:

```
php vendor/bin/doctrine.php orm:schema-tool:create
```

The following text must be printed in the terminal:

ATTENTION: This operation should not be executed in a production environment.

Creating database schema...

Database schema created successfully!

A new table called `Post` has been created in the database. You can use the SQLite client to show the structure of the generated table:

```
sqlite3 data/blog.db ".schema Post"
```

It should return the following query:

```
CREATE TABLE Post (id INTEGER NOT NULL, title VARCHAR(255) NOT
    NULL, body CLOB NOT NULL, publicationDate DATETIME NOT NULL,
    PRIMARY KEY(id));
CREATE INDEX publication_date_idx ON Post (publicationDate);
```

The following screenshot is the structure of the table Post:

Column ID	Name	Type	Not Null	Default Value	Primary Key	
0	id	INTEGER	1	null	1	
1	title	VARCHAR(255)	1	null	0	
2	body	CLOB	1	null	0	
3	publicationDate	DATETIME	1	null	0	

Doctrine is also able to generate the schema for MySQL and other supported DBMS. If we configure our app to use a MySQL server as a DBMS and we run the same command, the generated table will look similar to the following screenshot:

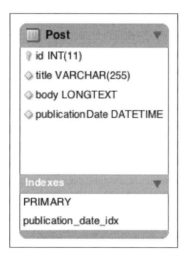

Installing Data fixtures

Fixtures are fake data that allow testing of an app without having to do the tedious task of manually creating data after each install. They are useful for automated testing processes and make it easier for a new developer to start working on our projects.

 Any application should be covered with automated tests. The blog app we are building is covered by Behat (http://behat.org/) tests. They are provided in downloads available on the Packt website.

Doctrine has an extension called Data Fixtures that ease fixtures creation. We will install it and use it to create some fake blog posts.

Type this command in the root of the project to install Doctrine Data Fixtures through Composer:

```
php composer.phar require doctrine/data-fixtures:1.0.*
```

The first step to using Doctrine Data Fixtures is to create a fixture class. Create a file called `LoadPostData.php` in the `src/Blog/DataFixtures` directory as shown in the following code:

```php
<?php

namespace Blog\DataFixtures;

use Blog\Entity\Post;
use Doctrine\Common\DataFixtures\FixtureInterface;
use Doctrine\Common\Persistence\ObjectManager;

/**
 * Post fixtures
 */
class LoadPostData implements FixtureInterface
{
  /**
   * Number of posts to add
   */
  const NUMBER_OF_POSTS = 10;

  /**
   * {@inheritDoc}
   */
  public function load(ObjectManager $manager)
  {
```

```
        for ($i = 1; $i <= self::NUMBER_OF_POSTS; $i++) {
            $post = new Post();
            $post

                setTitle(sprintf('Blog post number %d', $i))
                setBody(<<<EOT
                  Lorem ipsum dolor sit amet, consectetur
                     adipiscing elit.EOT
                )
                setPublicationDate(new \DateTime(sprintf('-%d
                  days', self::NUMBER_OF_POSTS - $i)))
            ;

            $manager->persist($post);
        }

        $manager->flush();
    }
}
```

This `LoadPostData` class contains the logic to create fake data. It creates ten blog posts with a generated title, a date of publication, and a text body.

The `LoadPostData` class implements the `load()` method defined in the `\Doctrine\ Common\DataFixtures\FixtureInterface` directory. This method takes in parameters for an `EntityManager` instance:

- Some reminders of *Chapter 1*, *Getting Started with Doctrine 2*: Calls to `EntityManager::persist()` sets the state of each new entity to managed
- The call to the `flush()` method, at the end of the process, will make Doctrine execute INSERT queries to effectively save data in the database

We still need to create a loader for our fixtures class. Create a file called `load-fixtures.php` in the `bin/` directory of your project with the following code:

```php
<?php

require_once __DIR__.'/../src/bootstrap.php';

use Doctrine\Common\DataFixtures\Loader;
use Doctrine\Common\DataFixtures\Purger\ORMPurger;
use Doctrine\Common\DataFixtures\Executor\ORMExecutor;

$loader = new Loader();
```

```
$loader->loadFromDirectory(__DIR__.'/../src/Blog/DataFixtures');

$purger = new ORMPurger();
$executor = new ORMExecutor($entityManager, $purger);
$executor->execute($loader->getFixtures());
```

In this utility, we initialize our app and get an Entity Manager as explained in *Chapter 1, Getting Started with Doctrine 2*. Then, we instantiate the fixtures loader provided by Doctrine Data Fixtures and tell it where to find our fixtures files.

We only have the `LoadPostData` class for now but we will create additional fixtures in the next chapters.

The `ORMExecutor` method is instanced and executed. It uses `ORMPurger` to erase existing data from the database. Then it populates the database with our fixtures.

Run the following command in the root directory of our project to load our fixtures:

```
php bin/load-fixtures.php
```

Our fixtures have been inserted in the database. Note that every time you run this command, all data in the database is permanently deleted.

Check that our database has been populated with the following command:

```
sqlite3 data/blog.db "SELECT * FROM Post;"
```

You should see ten rows similar to the following:

1 | Blog post number 1 | Lorem ipsum dolor sit amet, consectetur adipiscing elit. | 2013-11-08 20:01:13

2 | Blog post number 2 | Lorem ipsum dolor sit amet, consectetur adipiscing elit. | 2013-11-09 20:01:13

Creating a simple UI

We will create a simple UI to deal with our posts. This interface will let us create, retrieve, update, and delete a blog post. You may have already guessed that we will use the Entity Manager to do that.

For concision and to focus on the Doctrine part, this UI will have many drawbacks. *It should not be used in any kind of production or public server.* The primary concerns are as follows:

- **Not secure at all**: Everyone can access everything, as there is no authentication system, no data validation, and no CSRF protection
- **Badly designed**: There is no separation of concerns, no use of an MVC-like pattern, no REST architecture, no object-oriented code, and so on.

And of course this will be... graphically minimalistic!

- Cross Site Request Forgery (CSRF): `http://en.wikipedia.org/wiki/Cross-site_request_forgery`
- Separation of concerns: `http://en.wikipedia.org/wiki/Separation_of_concerns`
- Model-View-Controller (MVC) meta-pattern: `http://en.wikipedia.org/wiki/Model-view-controller`
- Representational state transfer (REST): `http://en.wikipedia.org/wiki/Representational_state_transfer`

For real-world apps, you should take a look at Symfony, a powerful framework that includes Doctrine and a ton of features (the validation component already presented, a form framework, a template engine, an internationalization system, and so on): `http://symfony.com/`

Listing posts

That being said, create the page that lists posts in the `web/index.php` file with the following code:

```php
<?php

/**
 * Lists all blog posts
 */

require_once __DIR__.'/../src/bootstrap.php';

/** @var $posts \Blog\Entity\Post[] Retrieve the list of all
  blog posts */
$posts = $entityManager->getRepository('Blog\Entity\Post')-
  >findAll();
```

```
?>

<!DOCTYPE html>
<html>
<head>
  <meta charset="utf-8">
  <title>My blog</title>
</head>
<body>
<h1>My blog</h1>

<?php foreach ($posts as $post): ?>
  <article>
      <h1>
          <?=htmlspecialchars($post->getTitle())?>
      </h1>
      Date of publication: <?=$post->getPublicationDate()-
        >format('Y-m-d H:i:s')?>

      <p>
          <?=nl2br(htmlspecialchars($post->getBody()))?>
      </p>

      <ul>
          <li>
              <a href="edit-post.php?id=<?=$post-
                >getId()?>">Edit this post</a>
          </li>
          <li>
              <a href="delete-post.php?id=<?=$post-
                >getId()?>">Delete this post</a>
          </li>
      </ul>
  </article>
<?php endforeach ?>
<?php if (empty($posts)): ?>
  <p>
      No post, for now!
  </p>
<?php endif ?>

<a href="edit-post.php">
  Create a new post
</a>
</html>
```

This first file is the main page of the blog. It lists all posts and display links to pages for creating, updating, or deleting posts.

After the app initialization, we get an `EntityManager` using the code we have written to configure Command-Line Tools in the first chapter.

We use this `EntityManager` to retrieve the repository of our `\Blog\Entity\Post` entities. For now, we use the default entity repository provided by Doctrine. We will learn more about them in *Chapter 4, Building Queries*. This default repository provides a `findAll()` method that retrieves a collection of all entities hydrated from the database.

> A `Collection` interface is similar to a regular PHP array (with some enhancements). This class is part of Doctrine Common:
> `http://www.doctrine-project.org/api/common/2.4/`
> `class-Doctrine.Common.Collections.Collection.html`

When calling it, Doctrine will query the database to find all rows of the `Post` table and populate a collection of `\Blog\Entity\Post` objects with the retrieved data. This collection is assigned to the `$posts` variable.

To browse this page, run the following command in the root directory of your project:

```
php -S localhost:8000 -t web/
```

This runs the built-in PHP webserver. Go to `http://localhost:8000` in your favorite web browser, and you'll see our ten fake posts.

> If it does not work, be sure that your PHP version is at least 5.4.

Creating and editing posts

It's time to create a page to add new blog posts. This same page will also allow editing an existing post. Put it in the `web/edit-post.php` file as shown in the following code:

```php
<?php

/**
 * Creates or edits a blog post
```

```php
    */

    use Blog\Entity\Post;

    require_once __DIR__.'/../src/bootstrap.php';

    // Retrieve the blog post if an id parameter exists
    if (isset ($_GET['id'])) {
      /** @var Post $post The post to edit */
      $post = $entityManager->find('Blog\Entity\Post',
        $_GET['id']);

      if (!$post) {
          throw new \Exception('Post not found');
      }
    }

    // Create or update the blog post
    if ('POST' === $_SERVER['REQUEST_METHOD']) {
      // Create a new post if a post has not been retrieved and set
        its date of publication
      if (!isset ($post)) {
          $post = new Post();
          // Manage the entity
          $entityManager->persist($post);

          $post->setPublicationDate(new \DateTime());
      }

      $post
          ->setTitle($_POST['title'])
          ->setBody($_POST['body'])
      ;

      // Flush changes to the database
      $entityManager->flush();

      // Redirect to the index
      header('Location: index.php');
      exit;
    }

    /** @var string Page title */
```

```php
$pageTitle = isset ($post) ? sprintf('Edit post #%d', $post-
  >getId()) : 'Create a new post';
?>
```

```html
<!DOCTYPE html>
<html>
<head>
  <meta charset="utf-8">
  <title><?=$pageTitle?> - My blog</title>
</head>
<body>
<h1>
  <?=$pageTitle?>
</h1>

<form method="POST">
  <label>
      Title
      <input type="text" name="title" value="<?=isset
        ($post) ? htmlspecialchars($post->getTitle()) : ''?>"
          maxlength="255" required>
  </label><br>

  <label>
      Body
      <textarea name="body" cols="20" rows="10"
        required><?=isset ($post) ? htmlspecialchars($post-
        >getBody()) : ''?></textarea>
  </label><br>

  <input type="submit">
</form>

<a href="index.php">Back to the index</a>
```

This page is a bit trickier:

- When called with an `id` parameter in the URL, it works on the `Post` entity with the given ID

 A best practice would be to use slugs instead of identifiers. They hide an application's internals, can be memorized by humans, and are better for Search Engine Optimization: http://en.wikipedia.org/wiki/Slug_(publishing).

- With no `id` parameter, it instantiates a new `Post` entity

- When called with the GET HTTP method, it displays a form populated with the current data of the `Post` in the case of an edit

- When called with the `Post` HTTP method (when the form is submitted), it creates or updates a `Post` entity, then redirects to the homepage of the blog

If an ID is provided through the URL, the `find()` method of the Entity Manager is used to retrieve the entity stored in the database with this ID. Doctrine queries the database and hydrates the entity for us.

If no `Post` with this ID is found, the NULL value is assigned to the `$post` variable instead of an instance of `\Blog\Entity\Post`. To avoid further errors, we throw an exception if this is the case. To find out more about PHP exceptions, refer to the website `http://php.net/manual/en/language.exceptions.php`.

Then, we call the `persist()` method of the Entity Manager with our new entity as a parameter. As explained in *Chapter 1, Getting Started with Doctrine 2*, this call to the `persist()` method sets the state of the entity to managed. It is necessary only for new entities because entities retrieved through Doctrine already have the managed state.

Next, we set the publication date of our newly created object. Thanks to the Doctrine mapping system, we just need to pass a `\DateTime` instance to the `setPublicationDate()` method and the ORM will convert it to the format needed by the DBMS for us (refer to the type correspondence table).

We also set the `$title` and `$body` properties using the fluent interface of getters and setters generated previously.

 If you don't know about fluent interface, read the following article: `http://martinfowler.com/bliki/FluentInterface.html`

When the call to the `flush()` method occurs, the Entity Manager tells Doctrine to synchronize all managed entities to the database. In this case, only our `Post` entity is managed. If it's a new entity, an INSERT SQL statement will be generated. If it's an existing entity, an UPDATE statement will be sent to the DBMS.

By default, Doctrine automatically wraps all operations done when the `EntityManager::flush()` method is called in a transaction. If an error occurs, the database state is restored as it was before the flush call (rollback).

This is usually the best option, but if you have specific needs, this auto-commit mode can be deactivated. This can be referred to at http://docs.doctrine-project. org/en/latest/reference/transactions-and-concurrency.html.

Deleting posts

Let's create a page to delete posts in the web/delete-post.php file:

```php
<?php

/**
 * Deletes a blog post
 */

require_once __DIR__.'/../src/bootstrap.php';

/** @var Post The post to delete */
$post = $entityManager->find('Blog\Entity\Post', $_GET['id']);
if (!$post) {
  throw new \Exception('Post not found');
}

// Delete the entity and flush
$entityManager->remove($post);
$entityManager->flush();

// Redirects to the index
header('Location: index.php');
exit;
```

We retrieve the post we want to delete using the ID parameter in the URL. We tell Doctrine to schedule it for removal with the call to the EntityManager::remove() method. After this call, the state of the entity is removed. When the flush() method is called, Doctrine executes a DELETE SQL query to remove data from the database.

 Note that after the call to the flush() method and the deletion from the database, the entity still exists in memory.

Summary

We now have a minimal but working blog app! Thanks to Doctrine, persisting, retrieving, and removing data to a database has never been so easy.

We have learned how to use annotations to map entity classes to database tables and rows, we generated a database schema without typing a line of SQL, we created fixtures and we used the Entity Manager to synchronize data with the database.

In the next chapter, we will learn how to map and manage One-To-One, One-To-Many/Many-To-One, and Many-To-Many associations between entities.

3
Associations

In the previous chapter, we learned how to use Doctrine annotations to add mapping information to an entity class. We used code and database schema generators provided by Doctrine command-line tools, and we created a minimalist blog software that uses an `EntityManager` class to create, update, delete, and display blog posts.

In the third chapter, we will learn how to handle associations between entities through the following topics:

- Getting started with the Doctrine associations
- Understanding the @ManyToOne and @OneToMany annotations with the comment system
- Understanding the @ManyToMany annotation with tags

Getting started with the Doctrine associations

We will specify Doctrine associations, such as other mapping information, using annotations (other methods such as XML and YAML configuration files are also supported. See *Chapter 2*, *Entities and Mapping Information*). Doctrine supports the following association types:

- **One-To-One**: One entity is linked to one entity
- **Many-To-One**: Several entities are linked to one entity (only available for bidirectional associations and always the inverse side of a One-To-Many association)
- **One-To-Many**: One entity is linked to several entities
- **Many-To-Many**: Several entities are linked to several entities

An association can be unidirectional or bidirectional. Unidirectional associations only have an owning side while bidirectional associations have both an owning side and an inverse side. In other words they can be explained as follows:

- A unidirectional association can be used in only one way: related entities are retrievable from the main entities. For example, a user has associated addresses. Addresses can be retrieved from the user, but the user cannot be retrieved from an address.

- A bidirectional association can be used in two ways: related entities are retrievable from main entities, and main entities are retrievable from related entities. For example, a user has associated orders. Orders can be retrieved from the user, and the user can be retrieved from an order.

Doctrine only manages the owning side of an association. This means that you always need to set the owning side; otherwise, if you only set the inverse side of an association, it will not be persisted with by the `EntityManager` class.

There is an easy way to identify the side of a bidirectional association. The owning side must have an `inversedBy` attribute, and the inverse side must have a `mappedBy` attribute. These attributes refer to the related entity class.

By default, One-To-One and Many-To-One associations are persisted with at the SQL level using a column storing the related ID and a foreign key. Many-To-Many associations always use an association table.

The names of columns and tables (if applicable) are generated automatically by Doctrine. Names can be changed using the `@JoinColumn` annotation, and the use of an association table can be forced with the `@JoinTable` annotation.

Understanding the @ManyToOne and @OneToMany annotations with the comment system

Let's start with the comments. Visitors to our blog should be able to react to our posts. We have to create a new `Comment` Doctrine entity type storing the reader's comments. `Comment` entities will be linked to one `Post` entity. One post can have many comments, and one comment is associated with a sole post.

The following E-R diagram represents the MySQL schema that will be generated using mapping information:

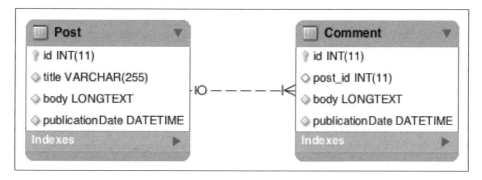

Creating the Comment entity class (owning side)

The Comment entity has the following four properties:

- id: This is a unique identifier of the comment
- body: This represents the comment's text
- publicationDate: This is the date of publication of the comment
- post_id: This represents the post related to the comment

Here is the first code snippet of the Comment entity, containing annotated properties. It must be placed in the Comment.php file at the src/Blog/Entity/ location.

```php
<?php

namespace Blog\Entity;

use Doctrine\ORM\Mapping\Entity;
use Doctrine\ORM\Mapping\Id;
use Doctrine\ORM\Mapping\GeneratedValue;
use Doctrine\ORM\Mapping\Column;
use Doctrine\ORM\Mapping\ManyToOne;

/**
 * Comment entity
 *
 * @Entity
 */
class Comment
```

```
{
    /**
     * @var int
     *
     * @Id
     * @GeneratedValue
     * @Column(type="integer")
     */
    protected $id;
    /**
     * @var string
     *
     * @Column(type="text")
     */
    protected $body;
    /**
     * @var \DateTime
     *
     * @Column(type="datetime")
     */
    protected $publicationDate;
    /**
     * @var Post
     *
     * @ManyToOne(targetEntity="Post", inversedBy="comments")
     */
    protected $post;
}
```

This entity class is similar to the `Post` entity class created in *Chapter 2, Entities and Mapping Information*. We use the `@ManyToOne` annotation to create a Many-To-One association between the `Comment` and `Post` entities. The related entity class is specified using the `targetEntity` attribute. This attribute is mandatory for every association.

To be able to retrieve comments directly from the `Post` entity, this association must be bidirectional. The `inversedBy` attribute marks this association as bidirectional and indicates the property of the `Post` entity class that owns the inverse side of this association. Here, this is the `$comments` property of `Post`.

 As for every entity class with `private` or `protected` properties, the `Comment` class must expose getters and setters to access them. We will generate getters and setters for every entity class of our app later in this chapter.

Adding the inverse side to the Post entity class

Now, we need to modify the Post entity class to add the inverse side of this association. The following steps need to be performed:

1. Open the Post.php file at the src/Blog/Entity/ location, and add the use statements from the previous code snippet:

   ```
   use Doctrine\ORM\Mapping\OneToMany;
   use Doctrine\Common\Collections\ArrayCollection;
   ```

2. Add the $comments property as shown in the following code snippet:

   ```
   /**
    * @var Comment[]
    *
    * @OneToMany(targetEntity="Comment", mappedBy="post")
    */
   protected $comments;
   ```

3. Add its initialization code in the constructor as shown in the next code snippet:

   ```
   /**
    * Initializes collections
    */
   public function __construct()
   {
       $this->comments = new ArrayCollection();
   }
   ```

4. Use the entity generator provided by Doctrine command-line tools to create getters and setters of the properties we have just added to the Comment and Post classes:

   ```
   php vendor/bin/doctrine.php orm:generate:entities src/
   ```

5. In the generated addComment() method, add the highlighted line of the following code snippet to automatically set the owning side of the association:

   ```
   public function addComment(\Blog\Entity\Comment
   $comments)
   {
       $this->comments[] = $comments;
       $comments->setPost($this);

       return $this;
   }
   ```

The $comments property holds the collection of comments associated with the Post entity. We use the @OneToMany annotation to mark this property as the inverse side of the association, defined earlier in the $post property of Comment. We have already explained the targetEntity attribute. The mappedBy attribute is an equivalent of the inversedBy attribute for the inverse side of an association. It indicates the property of the related entity class owning the other side of the association.

To allow Doctrine to manage the collection of elements properly, a special class provided by the Doctrine Common component must be used. The $comments property of the Post entity is initialized in the constructor as an instance of Doctrine\Common\Collections\ArrayCollection. ArrayCollection implements the Doctrine\Common\Collections\Collection interface. This will enable Doctrine to populate and manage the collection.

Doctrine Collection class implements the Countable, IteratorAggregate, and ArrayAccess interfaces (these interfaces are predefined in PHP or in the SPL). With that, Doctrine collections can be used like the standard PHP arrays and iterated transparently in the foreach loops.

More information about predefined interfaces and interfaces provided by the Standard PHP Library (SPL) can be found in the following PHP manual:

http://php.net/manual/en/reserved.interfaces.php
and http://php.net/manual/en/spl.interfaces.php

The addComment() and removeComment() methods generated by Doctrine command-line tools demonstrate the ways to use the methods of a Doctrine Collection class to add and remove items.

The full list of available methods is documented on the Doctrine website as follows:

http://docs.doctrine-project.org/en/latest/
reference/working-with-associations.html

Another important thing, as already explained, is that Doctrine only manages the owning side of an association. This is why we call the setPost() method of the Comment entity in the addComment() method. This allows persisting with an association from the inverse side.

This works only if the change-tracking policy of the entity is Deferred Implicit (This is the case by default). The deferred implicit policy is the most convenient one to use but can have negative effects on performance.

Again, refer to the Doctrine documentation at the following website to learn more about the different change-tracking policies that can be used:

`http://docs.doctrine-project.org/en/latest/reference/change-tracking-policies.html`

In a moment, we will update our UI to add the comment feature. First the database schema must be updated.

Updating the database schema

As with other annotations, Doctrine is able to automatically create the columns and foreign keys needed to store associations at the SQL layer. Run the `orm:schema-tool:update` command again bundled with the command-line tools as follows:

`php vendor/bin/doctrine.php orm:schema-tool:update --force`

Doctrine will automatically detect changes done to the mapping and will update the SQL schema accordingly. The `--force` flag can be added to effectively execute queries.

The `orm:schema-tool:update` command must not be used in production. It can permanently delete data (when columns are dropped for instance). Instead, the Doctrine Migrations library should be used to properly handle complicated migrations. Even if this library is not considered stable yet, it is very convenient. We can find this library at the following website:

`http://docs.doctrine-project.org/projects/doctrine-migrations/en/latest/reference/introduction.html`

Adding fixtures for the comments

As for posts, we will create some fixtures for the comments. Create a new file, LoadCommentData.php in the src/Blog/DataFixtures/ location. The next code snippet is used for this purpose:

```php
<?php

namespace Blog\DataFixtures;

use Blog\Entity\Comment;
use Doctrine\Common\DataFixtures\DependentFixtureInterface;
use Doctrine\Common\DataFixtures\Doctrine;
use Doctrine\Common\DataFixtures\FixtureInterface;
use Doctrine\Common\Persistence\ObjectManager;

/**
 * Comment fixtures
 */
class LoadCommentData implements FixtureInterface,
DependentFixtureInterface
{
    /**
     * Number of comments to add by post
     */
    const NUMBER_OF_COMMENTS_BY_POST = 5;

    /**
     * {@inheritDoc}
     */
    public function load(ObjectManager $manager)
    {
        $posts = $manager->getRepository('Blog\Entity\Post')-
>findAll();

        foreach ($posts as $post) {
            for ($i = 1; $i <= self::NUMBER_OF_COMMENTS_BY_POST;
            $i++) {
                $comment = new Comment();
                $comment
                    ->setBody(<<<EOT
Lorem ipsum dolor sit amet, consectetur adipiscing elit.
EOT
                    )
                    ->setPublicationDate(new \DateTime(sprintf('-%d
```

```
days', self::NUMBER_OF_COMMENTS_BY_POST - $i)))
                    ->setPost($post)
            ;

            $manager->persist($comment);
        }
    }

    $manager->flush();
}

/**
 * {@inheritDoc}
 */
public function getDependencies()
{
    return ['Blog\DataFixtures\LoadPostData'];
}
}
```

We use the `EntityManager` class to retrieve the `Post` entity repository, and then we use this repository to retrieve all the posts. We add five comments to each post. This data fixture class implements the `Doctrine\Common\DataFixtures\ DependentFixtureInterface` interface (the `getDependencies()` method). It tells the data loader to load `LoadPostData` first because this data fixture class is dependent on it.

Listing and creating comments

It's time to update the UI. Create a file, `view-post.php` in the `web/` location. This page displays a single post with all its comments and a form to add a new comment, and handles the comment creation.

The code to retrieve the post and handle the comment creation is as follows:

```php
<?php

/**
 * View a blog post
 */

use Blog\Entity\Comment;

require_once __DIR__ . '/../src/bootstrap.php';
```

```php
/** @var \Blog\Entity\Post $post The post to edit */
$post = $entityManager->find('Blog\Entity\Post', $_GET['id']);

if (!$post) {
    throw new \Exception('Post not found');
}

// Add a comment
if ('POST' === $_SERVER['REQUEST_METHOD']) {
    $comment = new Comment();
    $comment
        ->setBody($_POST['body'])
        ->setPublicationDate(new \DateTime())
        ->setPost($post)
    ;

    $entityManager->persist($comment);
    $entityManager->flush();

    header(sprintf('Location: view-post.php?id=%d', $post-
    >getId()));
    exit;
}
?>
```

As you can see, managing simple associations with Doctrine is easy. Setting a relation is as simple as calling a setter with the entity to the link in the parameter. Related entities are accessible using getters. The code to display details of the post, associated comments, and a form to publish a new comment (put it at the bottom of the same file) is as follows:

```html
<!DOCTYPE html>
<html>
<head>
    <meta charset="utf-8">
    <title><?=htmlspecialchars($post->getTitle())?> - My blog</title>
</head>
<body>

<article>
    <h1>
        <?=htmlspecialchars($post->getTitle())?>
```

```
    </h1>
    Date of publication: <?=$post->getPublicationDate()-
    >format('Y-m-d H:i:s')?>
    <p>
        <?=nl2br(htmlspecialchars($post->getBody()))?>
    </p>
    <?php if (count($post->getComments())): ?>
        <h2>Comments</h2>

        <?php foreach ($post->getComments() as $comment): ?>
            <article>
                <?=$comment->getPublicationDate()->format('Y-m-d
                H:i:s')?>

                <p><?=htmlspecialchars($comment->getBody())?></p>

                <a href="delete-comment.php?id=<?=$comment-
                >getId()?>">Delete this comment</a>
            </article>
        <?php endforeach ?>
    <?php endif ?>

    <form method="POST">
        <h2>Post a comment</h2>

        <label>
            Comment
            <textarea name="body"></textarea>
        </label><br>

        <input type="submit">
    </form>
</article>

<a href="index.php">Back to the index</a>
```

By default, Doctrine lazyloads the associated entities. It means that, in our example, Doctrine sends a first query to the DBMS to retrieve the post and then another to retrieve associated comments when getComments() is called. The benefit is that the query to retrieve the associated comments is never executed if the getComments() method is not called. But when the associated comments are always fetched, this is a useless overhead.

To make the lazyloading feature work, Doctrine internally wraps the entities into proxy classes. Proxy classes are responsible for getting the data of associated entities not already loaded from the database, when requested. Some details about that can be found at:

```
http://docs.doctrine-project.org/en/latest/reference/
working-with-objects.html#entity-object-graph-
traversal
```

We can change this behavior by setting a `fetch` attribute on the association annotation. This attribute can take the following values:

- `EAGER`: The related entities are generally fetched in the first query using a SQL join.
- `LAZY`: The related entities are fetched only if requested with another SQL query. This is the default value.
- `EXTRA_LAZY`: This allows performing some operations such as counting on collections that are not already fetched without loading the entire collection in the memory. To learn more about this topic, consult the following tutorial:

```
http://docs.doctrine-project.org/en/latest/tutorials/extra-
lazy-associations.html
```

Another way to eagerload the related entities is to use the Doctrine Query Builder to customize the generated request. We will demonstrate the power of the Query Builder in *Chapter 4, Building Queries*.

By deleting comments in the `view-post.php` page, we have created a link allowing the deletion of comments. The code to put in the `delete-comment.php` file in the `web/` location to make this feature work is as follows:

```php
<?php

/**
 * Deletes a comment
 */

require_once __DIR__ . '/../src/bootstrap.php';
```

```
/** @var Comment $comment The comment to delete */
$comment = $entityManager->find('Blog\Entity\Comment', $_GET['id']);

if (!$comment) {
    throw new \Exception('Comment not found');
}

// Delete the entity and flush
$entityManager->remove($comment);
$entityManager->flush();

// Redirect to the blog post
header(sprintf('Location: view-post.php?id=%d', $comment-
>getPost()->getId()));
exit;
```

This file is very similar to the `delete-post.php` file in the `web/` location created in *Chapter 1, Getting Started with Doctrine 2*. It retrieves the repository through the `EntityManager` class, uses it to retrieve the comment to delete, calls `remove()`, and persists with the change to DBMS with `flush()`.

Updating the index

Update the `index.php` file in the `web/` location to create a link to the new, detailed post view as shown in the following code:

```
<h1>
    <?=htmlspecialchars($post->getTitle())?>
</h1>
```

To make our comment feature ready, replace the preceding code with the following code:

```
<h1>
    <a href="view-post.php?id=<?=$post->getId()?>">
        <?=htmlspecialchars($post->getTitle())?>
    </a>
</h1>
```

Understanding the @ManyToMany annotation with tags

Tags group posts by topics. A tag contains several posts, and a post has several tags. This is a Many-To-Many bidirectional association. Doctrine manages transparently the association table needed to store Many-To-Many relations at the SQL level. The MySQL schema that will be generated is shown in the following screenshot:

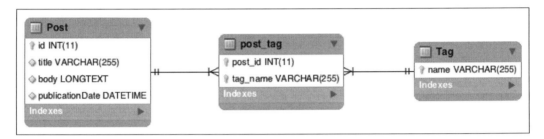

Creating the Tag entity class (inverse side)

The Tag entity class has only two properties:

- name: This is the name of the tag, it is unique, and is the identifier of the entity
- posts: This is the collection of posts associated with this tag

The following are the steps to create the Tag entity class:

1. Create a Tag.php file in the src/Blog/Entity/ location that contains the entity class using the following code snippet:

```php
<?php

namespace Blog\Entity;

use Doctrine\Common\Collections\ArrayCollection;
use Doctrine\ORM\Mapping\Entity;
use Doctrine\ORM\Mapping\Column;
use Doctrine\ORM\Mapping\Id;
use Doctrine\ORM\Mapping\ManyToMany;

/**
 * Tag entity
 *
 * @Entity
```

```
    */
    class Tag
    {
        /**
         * @var string
         *
         * @Id
         * @Column(type="string")
         */
        protected $name;
        /**
         * @var Post[]
         *
         * @ManyToMany(targetEntity="Post", mappedBy="tags")
         */
        protected $posts;

        /**
         * Initializes collection
         */
        public function __construct()
        {
            $this->posts = new ArrayCollection();
        }

        /**
         * String representation
         *
         * @return string
         */
        public function __toString()
        {
            return $this->getName();
        }
    }
```

2. Generate getters and setters using the following command:

   php vendor/bin/doctrine.php orm:generate:entities src/

3. Add the following line of code to set the owning side of the association after
   $this->posts[] = $posts; in the addPost() method:

   $posts->addTag($this);

The property $name is the identifier of the Tag entity. Unlike the Post and Comment entities, its value is not automatically generated by DBMS; it's the name of the tag. That's why the @GeneratedValue annotation is not used here. The name of the tag must be unique and must be set by the application.

The @ManyToMany annotation is used to mark the association. The meanings of the targetEntity and mappedBy attributes are the same as for the @OneToMany annotation. The @ManyToMany annotation accepts a mappedBy attribute for the inverse side and inversedBy for the owning side. The owning side of this association is on the Post entity. As for any Doctrine collection, the $posts property is initialized in the constructor. We also create a __toString() method returning the name of the tag to be able to cast instances of Tag to the string.

The __toString() magic method allows us to convert an object to a string. For more details we can refer to the following link:

http://www.php.net/manual/en/language.oop5.magic.php#object.tostring

Updating the Post entity class (owning side)

Modify the Post.php file in the src/Blog/Entity/ location to add the owning side of the association using the following steps:

1. Add the following use statements:

```
use Doctrine\ORM\Mapping\ManyToMany;
use Doctrine\ORM\Mapping\JoinTable;
use Doctrine\ORM\Mapping\JoinColumn;
```

2. Add the mapped property using the following code snippet:

```
/**
 * @var Tag[]
 *
 * @ManyToMany(targetEntity="Tag", inversedBy="posts",
 fetch="EAGER", cascade={"persist"}, orphanRemoval=true)
 * @JoinTable(
 *      inverseJoinColumns={@JoinColumn(name="tag_name",
 referencedColumnName="name")}
 * )
 */
protected $tags;
```

3. Initialize the property in the constructor as shown in the following code snippet:

```
public function __construct()
{
    // …
    $this->tags = new ArrayCollection();
}
```

4. To generate getters and setters, you can use the following command:

php vendor/bin/doctrine.php orm:generate:entities src/

Two new attributes of the @ManyToMany annotation are introduced here, that is, cascade and orphanRemoval.

By default, the associated entities are not automatically set to the managed state when the main entity is set. This must be done manually with a call to the persist() method of the EntityManager class for each associated entity. If the cascade attribute is used with persist as value, the related entities will be automatically persisted with when the main entity is persisted with.

Here, the related tags will be persisted with when the Post entity is persisted with. The cascade attribute can take other values, the most useful of which is remove. When remove is used, the related entities will be deleted when the main entity is deleted.

The CASCADE operations are handled in memory by **Object Relational Mapper (ORM)**. They are not equivalent to the SQL DELETE CASCADE operations and can use a lot of memory. They should be used with parsimony to preserve the performance of the application.

The SQL DELETE CASCADE operations can be added through the onDelete attribute of the @JoinColumn annotation.

With the orphanRemoval attribute set to true, Doctrine will automatically delete the entities not linked with the main entity anymore. If the Tag entity is removed from the $tags collection of a Post entity, and this Post entity was the only one linked to the Tag entity, the Tag entity will be permanently deleted.

The fetch attribute has already been explained earlier in the chapter. With the EAGER value, it tells Doctrine to automatically retrieve the related tags with a JOIN query when the posts are retrieved. This is useful in the context of our app because the tags of the Post entity are displayed every time the post is displayed.

Because the identifier of Tag is not marked with the @GeneratedValue annotation, Doctrine will not be able to guess it. The @JoinTable and @JoinColumn annotations are here to override the default behavior.

We set a custom `JOIN` column with `@JoinColumn` for the tag-related side of the association (inverse side) through the `inverseJoinColumns` attribute of `@JoinTable`. The `referencedColumnName` attribute of `@JoinColumn` tells Doctrine to look for the `$name` property (instead of `$id` by default) for the identifier of `Tag`. The `name` attribute sets the name of the column holding the identifier of `Tag` in the SQL level association table to `tag_name` (instead of `tag_id` by default).

Updating the schema again

It's time to update the SQL schema again to match our changes. We use the following command on the command line:

```
php vendor/bin/doctrine.php orm:schema-tool:update --force
```

Creating tag fixtures

Create a `LoadTagData.php` file at `src/Blog/DataFixtures/`, which contains tag fixtures using the following code snippet:

```php
<?php

namespace Blog\DataFixtures;

use Blog\Entity\Tag;
use Doctrine\Common\DataFixtures\DependentFixtureInterface;
use Doctrine\Common\DataFixtures\Doctrine;
use Doctrine\Common\DataFixtures\FixtureInterface;
use Doctrine\Common\Persistence\ObjectManager;

/**
 * Tag fixtures
 */
class LoadTagData implements FixtureInterface,
DependentFixtureInterface
{
    /**
     * Number of comments to add by post
     */
    const NUMBER_OF_TAGS = 5;
```

```php
/**
 * {@inheritDoc}
 */
public function load(ObjectManager $manager)
{
    $tags = [];
    for ($i = 1; $i <= self::NUMBER_OF_TAGS; $i++) {
        $tag = new Tag();
        $tag->setName(sprintf("tag%d", $i));

        $tags[] = $tag;
    }

    $posts = $manager->getRepository('Blog\Entity\Post')-
    >findAll();

    $tagsToAdd = 1;
    foreach ($posts as $post) {
        for ($j = 0; $j < $tagsToAdd; $j++) {
            $post->addTag($tags[$j]);
        }

        $tagsToAdd = $tagsToAdd % 5 + 1;
    }

    $manager->flush();
}

/**
 * {@inheritDoc}
 */
public function getDependencies()
{
    return ['Blog\DataFixtures\LoadPostData'];
}
}
```

Thanks to the `persist` attribute, we can add tags to posts without manually persisting with them.

After the fixtures, we have to update the UI.

Managing the tags of a post

Edit the `edit-post.php` file at the `web/` location, and add the code to manage the tags with the following steps:

1. Add the following `use` statement at the top of the file:

    ```
    use Blog\Entity\Tag;
    ```

2. Find the following code snippet:

    ```
    $post
        ->setTitle($_POST['title'])
        ->setBody($_POST['body'])
    ;
    ```

3. Add this code after to `extract` and manage the submitted tags:

    ```
    $newTags = [];
    foreach (explode(',', $_POST['tags']) as $tagName) {
        $trimmedTagName = trim($tagName);
        $tag = $entityManager->find('Blog\Entity\Tag',
        $trimmedTagName);
        if (!$tag) {
            $tag = new Tag();
            $tag->setName($trimmedTagName);
        }

        $newTags[] = $tag;
    }

    // Removes unused tags
    foreach (array_diff($post->getTags()->toArray(),
    $newTags) as $tag) {
        $post->removeTag($tag);
    }

    // Adds new tags
    foreach (array_diff($newTags, $post->getTags()-
    >toArray()) as $tag) {
        $post->addTag($tag);
    }
    ```

4. Find the following code snippet:

    ```
    <label>
        Body
        <textarea name="body" cols="20" rows="10"
        required><?=isset ($post) ? htmlspecialchars($post-
    ```

```
>getBody()) : ''?></textarea>
</label><br>
```

5. Add the following form widget after `to display` and update the tags:

```
<label>
    Tags
    <input type="text" name="tags" value="<?=isset
    ($post) ? htmlspecialchars(implode(', ', $post-
    >getTags()->toArray())) : ''?>" required>
</label><br>
```

Each tag name is extracted from the submitted string. The corresponding `Tag` entity is retrieved from the repository or created if not found.

Thanks to its `toArray()` method, the `tag` collection of the `Post` object is converted to a standard PHP array.

The standard `array_diff()` function is used to identify removed and added `Tag` objects. The arguments of `array_diff()` must be arrays of objects that can be converted to a string. It is okay here because our `Tag` class implements the `__toString()` magic method.

Deleted tags are removed through the `Post::removeTag()` function, and new tags are added through `Post::addTag()`.

Thanks to the `CASCADE` attribute defined in the `Post` entity class, we don't need to persist individually with each new tag.

In the template, the tag list is transformed to a string following the pattern "tagname1, tagname2, tagname3".

Summary

In this chapter, we have learned how to manage all types of associations supported by the Doctrine ORM. We learned about unidirectional and bidirectional associations and the concept of owning side and inverse side. We also used what we have learned in previous chapters, especially the `EntityManager` class, the fixture loader, and generators.

In the next chapter, we will learn how to create complex queries with DQL and Query Builder.

Thanks to them, we will create lists of posts grouped by their tags. We will also take a look at the aggregate functions.

4
Building Queries

In the previous chapter, we added commenting and tagging support to our blog software. Although it works fine, some of the features can be enhanced.

In this chapter, we will leverage some very important parts of Doctrine: **Doctrine Query Language (DQL)**, entity repositories, and the Query Builder. We will cover the following aspects in this chapter:

- Optimizing the Comment feature
- Creating a page to filter the posts with the help of tags
- Displaying the number of comments of a post on the home page

Understanding DQL

DQL is the acronym of Doctrine Query Language. It's a domain-specific language that is very similar to SQL, but is not SQL. Instead of querying the database tables and rows, DQL is designed to query the object model's entities and mapped properties.

DQL is inspired by and similar to HQL, the query language of Hibernate, a popular ORM for Java. For more details you can visit this website: http://www.hibernate.org/.

 Learn more about domain-specific languages at: http://en.wikipedia.org/wiki/Domain-specific_language

To better understand what it means, let's run our first DQL query.

Doctrine command-line tools are as genuine as a Swiss Army knife. They include a command called `orm:run-dql` that runs the DQL query and displays it's result. Use it to retrieve `title` and all the comments of the post with `1` as an identifier:

```
php vendor/bin/doctrine.php orm:run-dql "SELECT p.title, c.body
FROM Blog\Entity\Post p JOIN p.comments c WHERE p.id=1"
```

It looks like a SQL query, but it's definitely not a SQL query. Examine the FROM and the JOIN clauses; they contain the following aspects:

- A fully qualified entity class name is used in the FROM clause as the root of the query

- All the Comment entities associated with the selected Post entities are joined, thanks to the presence of the comments property of the Post entity class in the JOIN clause

As you can see, data from the entities associated with the main entity can be requested in an object-oriented way. Properties holding the associations (on the owning or the inverse side) can be used in the JOIN clause.

Despite some limitations (especially in the field of subqueries), which we will see how to get around in *Chapter 5, Going Further*, DQL is a powerful and flexible language to retrieve object graphs. Internally, Doctrine parses the DQL queries, generates and executes them through **Database Abstraction Layer (DBAL)** corresponding to the SQL queries, and hydrates the data structures with results.

Until now, we only used Doctrine to retrieve the PHP objects. Doctrine is able to hydrate other types of data structures, especially arrays and basic types. It's also possible to write custom hydrators to populate any data structure.

If you look closely at the return of the previous call of `orm:run-dql`, you'll see that it's an array, and not an object graph, that has been hydrated.

As with all the topics covered in this book, more information about built-in hydration modes and custom hydrators is available in the Doctrine documentation on the following website:

```
http://docs.doctrine-project.org/en/latest/reference/
dql-doctrine-query-language.html#hydration-modes
```

Using the entity repositories

Entity repositories are classes responsible for accessing and managing entities. Just like entities are related to the database rows, entity repositories are related to the database tables.

We have already used default entity repositories provided by Doctrine to retrieve the entities in the previous chapters. All the DQL queries should be written in the entity repository related to the entity type they retrieve. It hides the ORM from other components of the application and makes it easier to re-use, refactor, and optimize the queries.

> Doctrine entity repositories are an implementation of the Table Data Gateway design pattern. For more details, visit the following website:
> `http://martinfowler.com/eaaCatalog/tableDataGateway.html`

A base repository, available for every entity, provides useful methods for managing the entities in the following manner:

- `find($id)`: It returns the entity with `$id` as an identifier or `null`

> It is used internally by the `find()` method of the Entity Managers. We used this shortcut many times in the previous chapters.

- `findAll()`: It retrieves an array that contains all the entities in this repository
- `findBy(['property1' => 'value', 'property2' => 1], ['property3' => 'DESC', 'property4' => 'ASC'])`: It retrieves an array that contains entities matching all the criteria passed in the first parameter and ordered by the second parameter
- `findOneBy(['property1' => 'value', 'property2' => 1])`: It is similar to `findBy()` but retrieves only the first entity or `null` if none of the entities match the criteria

Entity repositories also provide shortcut methods that allow a single property to filter entities. They follow this pattern: `findBy*()` and `findOneBy*()`.

For instance, calling `findByTitle('My title')` is equivalent to calling `findBy(['title' => 'My title'])`.

This feature uses the magical `__call()` PHP method. For more details visit the following website:

`http://php.net/manual/en/language.oop5.overloading.php#object.call`

As seen in *Chapter 3, Associations*, these shortcut methods don't join the related entities unless we add a `fetch="EAGER"` attribute to the association annotation in the entity class. Another SQL query will be issued if (and only if) a related entity (or a collection of entities) is requested through a method call.

In our blog app, we want to display comments in the detailed post view, but it is not necessary to fetch them from the list of posts. Eager loading through the `fetch` attribute is not a good choice for the list, and Lazy loading slows down the detailed view.

A solution to this would be to create a custom repository with extra methods for executing our own queries. We will write a custom method that collates comments in the detailed view.

Creating custom entity repositories

Custom entity repositories are classes extending the base entity repository class provided by Doctrine. They are designed to receive custom methods that run the DQL queries.

As usual, we will use the mapping information to tell Doctrine to use a custom repository class. This is the role of the `repositoryClass` attribute of the `@Entity` annotation.

Kindly perform the following steps to create a custom entity repository:

1. Reopen the `Post.php` file at the `src/Blog/Entity/` location and add a `repositoryClass` attribute to the existing `@Entity` annotation like the following line of code:

   `@Entity(repositoryClass="PostRepository")`

2. Doctrine command-line tools also provide an entity repository generator. Type the following command to use it:

```
php vendor/bin/doctrine.php orm:generate:repositories src/
```

3. Open this new empty custom repository, which we just generated in the `PostRepository.phpPostRepository.php` file, at the `src/Blog/Entity/` location. Add the following method for retrieving the posts and comments:

```
/**
 * Finds a post with its comments
 *
 * @param  int   $id
 * @return Post
 */
public function findWithComments($id)
{
    return $this
        ->createQueryBuilder('p')
        ->addSelect('c')
        ->leftJoin('p.comments', 'c')
        ->where('p.id = :id')
        ->orderBy('c.publicationDate', 'ASC')
        ->setParameter('id', $id)
        ->getQuery()
        ->getOneOrNullResult()
    ;
}
```

Our custom repository extends the default entity repository provided by Doctrine. The standard methods, described earlier in the chapter, are still available.

Getting started with Query Builder

`QueryBuilder` is an object designed to help build the DQL queries through a PHP API with a fluent interface (to find out more about fluent interfaces, see *Chapter 2, Entities and Mapping Information*). It allows us to retrieve the generated DQL queries through the `getDql()` method (useful for debugging) or directly use the `Query` object (provided by Doctrine).

To increase performance, QueryBuilder caches the generated DQL queries and manages an internal state.

The full API and states of the DQL query are documented on the following website:

http://docs.doctrine-project.org/projects/doctrine-orm/en/latest/reference/query-builder.html

We will give an in-depth explanation of the findWithComments() method that we created in the PostRepository class.

Firstly, a QueryBuilder instance is created with the createQueryBuilder() method inherited from the base entity repository. The QueryBuilder instance takes a string as a parameter. This string will be used as an alias of the main entity class. By default, all the fields of the main entity class are selected and no other clauses except SELECT and FROM are populated.

The leftJoin() call creates a JOIN clause that retrieves comments associated with the posts. Its first argument is the property to join and its second is the alias; these will be used in the query for the joined entity class (here, the letter c will be used as an alias for the Comment class).

Unless the SQL JOIN clause is used, the DQL query automatically fetches the entities associated with the main entity. There is no need for keywords like ON or USING. Doctrine automatically knows whether a join table or a foreign-key column must be used.

The addSelect() call appends comment data to the SELECT clause. The alias of the entity class is used to retrieve all the fields (this is similar to the * operator in SQL). As in the first DQL query of this chapter, specific fields can be retrieved with the notation alias.propertyName.

You guessed it, the call to the where() method sets the WHERE part of the query.

Under the hood, Doctrine uses prepared SQL statements. They are more efficient than the standard SQL queries.

The id parameter will be populated by the value set by the call to setParameter().

Thanks again to prepared statements and this setParameter() method, SQL Injection attacks are automatically avoided.

SQL Injection Attacks are a way to execute malicious SQL queries using user inputs that have not escaped. Let's take the following example of a bad DQL query to check if a user has a specific role:

```
$query = $entityManager->createQuery('SELECT ur FROM
UserRole ur WHERE ur.username = "' . $username . '" AND
ur.role = "' . $role . '"');
$hasRole = count($query->getResult());
```

This DQL query will be translated into SQL by Doctrine. If someone types the following username:

```
" OR "a"="a
```

the SQL code contained in the string will be injected and the query will always return some results. The attacker has now gained access to a private area.

The proper way should be to use the following code:

```
$query = $entityManager->createQuery("SELECT ur FROM
UserRole WHERE username = :username and role = :role");
$query->setParameters([
    'username' => $username,
    'role' => $role
]);
$hasRole = count($query->getResult());
```

Thanks to prepared statements, special characters (like quotes) contained in the username are not dangerous, and this snippet will work as expected.

The `orderBy()` call generates an ORDER BY clause that orders results as per the publication date of the comments, older first.

Most SQL instructions also have an object-oriented equivalent in DQL. The most common join types can be made using DQL; they generally have the same name.

The `getQuery()` call tells the Query Builder to generate the DQL query (if needed, it will get the query from its cache if possible), to instantiate a Doctrine `Query` object, and to populate it with the generated DQL query.

This generated DQL query will be as follows:

```
SELECT p, c FROM Blog\Entity\Post p LEFT JOIN p.comments c WHERE
p.id = :id ORDER BY c.publicationDate ASC
```

The Query object exposes another useful method for the purpose of debugging: getSql(). As its name implies, getSql() returns the SQL query corresponding to the DQL query, which Doctrine will run on DBMS. For our DQL query, the underlying SQL query is as follows:

```
SELECT p0_.id AS id0, p0_.title AS title1, p0_.body AS body2,
p0_.publicationDate AS publicationDate3, c1_.id AS id4, c1_.body
AS body5, c1_.publicationDate AS publicationDate6, c1_.post_id AS
post_id7 FROM Post p0_ LEFT JOIN Comment c1_ ON p0_.id =
c1_.post_id WHERE p0_.id = ? ORDER BY c1_.publicationDate ASC
```

The getOneOrNullResult() method executes it, retrieves the first result, and returns it as a Post entity instance (this method returns null if no result is found).

Like the QueryBuilder object, the Query object manages an internal state to generate the underlying SQL query only when necessary.

Performance is something to be very careful about while using Doctrine. When set in production mode (see *Chapter 1, Getting Started with Doctrine 2*), ORM is able to cache the generated queries (DQL through the QueryBuilder objects, SQL through the Query objects) and results of the queries.

ORM must be configured to use one of the blazing, fast, supported systems (APC, Memcache, XCache, or Redis) as shown on the following website:

http://docs.doctrine-project.org/en/latest/
reference/caching.html

We still need to update the view layer to take care of our new findWithComments() method.

Open the view-post.php file at the web/location, where you will find the following code snippet:

```
$post = $entityManager->getRepository('Blog\Entity\Post')->find
($_GET['id']);
```

Replace the preceding line of code with the following code snippet:

```
$post = $entityManager->getRepository('Blog\Entity\Post')-
>findWithComments($_GET['id']);
```

Filtering by tag

To discover a more advanced use of the QueryBuilder and DQL, we will create a list of posts having one or more tags.

Tag filtering is good for Search Engine Optimization and allows the readers to easily find the content they are interested in. We will build a system that is able to list posts that have several tags in common; for example, all the posts tagged with Doctrine and Symfony.

To filter our posts using tags kindly perform the following steps:

1. Add another method to our custom `PostRepository` class (`src/Blog/Entity/PostRepository.php`) using the following code:

    ```
    /**
     * Finds posts having tags
     *
     * @param string[] $tagNames
     * @return Post[]
     */
    public function findHavingTags(array $tagNames)
    {
        return $queryBuilder = $this
            ->createQueryBuilder('p')
                ->addSelect('t')
            ->join('p.tags', 't')
            ->where('t.name IN (:tagNames)')
            ->groupBy('p.id')
            ->having('COUNT(t.name) >= :numberOfTags')
            ->setParameter('tagNames', $tagNames)
            ->setParameter('numberOfTags',
            count($tagNames))
            ->getQuery()
            ->getResult()
        ;
    }
    ```

    This method is a bit more complex. It takes in a parameter as an array of tag names and returns an array of posts that has all these tags.

    The query deserves some explanation, which is as follows:

    ○   The main entity class (automatically set by the inherited `createQueryBuilder()` method) is `Post` and its alias is the letter `p`.

    ○   We join the associated tags through a `JOIN` clause; the `Tag` class is aliased by `t`.

- Thanks to `where()` being called, we retrieve only the posts tagged by one of the tags passed in the parameter. We use an awesome feature of Doctrine that allows us to directly use an array as a query parameter.

- Results of `where()` are grouped by `id` with the call to `groupBy()`.

- We use the aggregate function `COUNT()` in the `HAVING` clause to filter the posts that are tagged by some tags of the `$tagNames` array, but not all of them.

2. Edit the `index.php` file in `web/` to use our new method. Here, you will find the following code:

```
/** @var $posts \Blog\Entity\Post[] Retrieve the list of
all blog posts */
$posts = $entityManager->getRepository('Blog\Entity\Post')-
>findAll();
```

And replace the preceding code with the next code snippet:

```
$repository = $entityManager-
>getRepository('Blog\Entity\Post');
/** @var $posts \Blog\Entity\Post[] Retrieve the list of
all blog posts */
$posts = isset($_GET['tags']) ? $repository-
>findHavingTags($_GET['tags']) : $repository->findAll();
```

Now, when a `GET` parameter called `tags` exists in the URL, it is used to filter posts. Better, if several comma-separated tags are passed in, only posts with all these tags will be displayed.

3. Type `http://localhost:8000/index.php?tags=tag4,tag5` in your favorite browser. Thanks to the fixtures we have created in the previous chapter, posts 5 and 10 should be listed.

4. In the same file, find the following code:

```
<p>
    <?=nl2br(htmlspecialchars($post->getBody()))?>
</p>
```

And add the list of tags as follows:

```
<ul>
<?php foreach ($post->getTags() as $tag): ?>
    <li>
        <a href="index.php?tags=<?=urlencode($tag)?>"><?=h
tmlspecialchars($tag)?></a>
    </li>
<?php endforeach ?>
</ul>
```

A smart list of tags with links to the tag page is displayed. You can copy this code and then paste it in the `view-post.php` file in the `web/` location; or better, *don't repeat yourself*: create a small helper function to display the tags.

Counting comments

We still need to make some cosmetic changes. Posts with a lot of comments interest many readers. It would be better if the number of comments for each post was available directly from the list page. Doctrine can populate an array containing the result of the call to an `aggregate` function as the first row and hydrated entities as the second.

Add the following method, for retrieving posts with the associated comments, to the `PostRepository` class:

```
/**
 * Finds posts with comment count
 *
 * @return array
 */
public function findWithCommentCount()
{
    return $this
        ->createQueryBuilder('p')
        ->leftJoin('p.comments', 'c')
        ->addSelect('COUNT(c.id)')
        ->groupBy('p.id')
        ->getQuery()
        ->getResult()
    ;
}
```

Thanks to the GROUP BY clause and the call to `addSelect()`, this method will return a two-dimensional array instead of an array of the Post entities. Arrays in the returned array contain two values, which are as follows:

- Our Post entity at the first index
- The result of the COUNT() function of DQL (the number of comments) at the second index

In the `index.php` file at the `web/` location, find the following code:

```
$posts = $repository->findHavingTags(explode(',',
$_GET['tags']));
} else {
    $posts = $repository->findAll();
}
```

And replace the preceding code with the following code to use our new method:

```
$results = $repository->findHavingTags(explode(',',
$_GET['tags']));
} else {
    $results = $repository->findWithCommentCount();
}
```

To match the new structure returned by `findWithCommentCount()`, find the following code:

```
<?php foreach ($posts as $post): ?>
```

And replace the preceding code with the next code snippet:

```
<?php
    foreach ($results as $result):
        $post = $result[0];
        $commentCount = $result[1];
?>
```

> As seen previously, the use of a custom hydrator is a better practice while handling such cases.
>
> You should also take a look at Custom AST Walker as shown on the following website:
>
> `http://docs.doctrine-project.org/en/latest/cookbook/dql-custom-walkers.html`

Find the following code snippet:

```
<?php if (empty($posts)): ?>
```

And replace the preceding code with the next code snippet:

```
<?php if (empty($results)): ?>
```

It's time to display the number of comments. Insert the following code after the tag list:

```php
<?php if ($commentCount == 0): ?>
    Be the first to comment this post.
<?php elseif ($commentCount == 1): ?>
    One comment
<?php else: ?>
    <?= $commentCount ?> comments
<?php endif ?>
```

As the `index.php` file at the `web/` location also uses the `findHavingTags()` method to display the list of tagged articles, we need to update this method too. This is done using the following code:

```php
// ...
->addSelect('t')
->addSelect('COUNT(c.id)')
->leftJoin('p.comments', 'c')
// ...
```

Summary

In this chapter, we have learned about DQL, its differences from SQL, and its Query Builder. We also learned about the concept of entity repositories and how to create custom ones.

Even if there is a lot more to learn from these topics and from Doctrine in general, our knowledge should be sufficient to start developing complete and complex applications using Doctrine as a persistent system.

In *Chapter 5*, *Going Further*, the last chapter of this book, we will go a step further and cover some more advanced topics, including how to handle inheritance, how to make native SQL queries, and the basics of the event system.

5
Going Further

In previous chapters we learned the basics of the Doctrine ORM. We are now able to create complex domain classes, generate underlying SQL tables, load data fixtures, and execute advanced queries. We know everything we need to know to develop the model layer of small web applications.

The library, however, provides more advanced features. In this chapter we will briefly cover various topics not addressed previously: inheritance, lifecycle callbacks, and native queries.

Implementing inheritance

Like all object-oriented programming languages, PHP is designed on top of the inheritance concept; however, relational databases are not. This is the common problem when mapping classes to tables.

The Doctrine ORM provides the following three ways to achieve inheritance:

- Mapped Superclasses
- Single Table Inheritance
- Class Table Inheritance

To learn about them, we will create three implementations of the same model, that is, for content authors.

Both posts and comments have authors. Authors must have a name and an e-mail address. Posts' authors (and only them) can also have an optional biography.

To represent this, we will create two classes: `PostAuthor` and `CommentAuthor`. They both extend an abstract `Author` class. Each `Comment` entity is linked to a `CommentAuthor` class and each `Post` entity to a `PostAuthor` class.

Using Mapped Superclasses

Mapped Superclasses are simple PHP classes that share mapped properties used by their descendant entities. Mapped Superclasses are not entities themselves. They are extended by entities.

Mapped Superclasses are never directly persisted to the database. They are not retrievable through the query builder and cannot be the inverse-side of an association.

They are like any other PHP class extended by entities, except that they can hold properties that will be persisted by their descendants.

> This type of inheritance is not well suited for this use case. Single Table Inheritance is better here.

1. Start by creating the Mapped Superclass. Create a new abstract class called `Author` in the `Author.php` file at the location `src/Blog/Entity/`as shown in the following code:

```php
<?php

namespace Blog\Entity;

use Doctrine\ORM\Mapping\MappedSuperclass;
use Doctrine\ORM\Mapping\Id;
use Doctrine\ORM\Mapping\GeneratedValue;
use Doctrine\ORM\Mapping\Column;

/**
 * Author superclass
 *
 * @MappedSuperclass
 */
abstract class Author
{
    /**
     * @var int
     *
     * @Id
     * @GeneratedValue
     * @Column(type="integer")
     */
    protected $id;
    /**
```

```
 * @var string
 *
 * @Column(type="string")
 */
protected $name;
/**
 * @var string
 *
 * @Column(type="string")
 */
protected $email;
}
```

Thanks to the `@MappedSuperclass` annotation, the mapped properties of the `Author` class inherited by `PostAuthor` and `CommentAuthor` classes will be taken into account by Doctrine.

2. Write getters for all the properties and setters for all except the `$id` instance.

 At the time of writing, Doctrine Command-Line Tools were not able to generate getters and setters for a Mapped Superclass and suffered a bug when generating getters and setters for child classes.

3. Create a `PostAuthor.php` file in the same directory that contains the `PostAuthor` class as shown in the following code:

```php
<?php

namespace Blog\Entity;

use Doctrine\Common\Collections\ArrayCollection;
use Doctrine\ORM\Mapping\Entity;
use Doctrine\ORM\Mapping\OneToMany;
use Doctrine\ORM\Mapping\Column;

/**
 * Post author entity
 *
 * @Entity
 */
class PostAuthor extends Author
{
    /**
     * @var string
     *
```

```
 * @Column(type="text", nullable=true)
 */
protected $bio;
/**
 * @var Post[]
 *
 * @OneToMany(targetEntity="Post", mappedBy="postAuthor")
 */
protected $posts;

/**
 * Initializes collections
 */
public function __construct()
{
    $this->posts = new ArrayCollection();
}
}
```

The PostAuthor entity class extends the Author Mapped Superclass. PostAuthor holds specific data of posts' authors: a bio property and a One-To-Many association to posts.

At the database level, a table called PostAuthor will be created with all the columns defined with the @Column annotation in Author and PostAuthor classes.

4. Write getters and setters for this class.

5. To make this association work, we need to add the code of the owning-side of the association to the src/Blog/Entity/Post.php file. To do this, add the following property:

```
/**
 * @var PostAuthor
 *
 * @ManyToOne(targetEntity="PostAuthor", inversedBy="posts")
 */
protected $author;
```

6. You guessed it! Write the getter and setter for the preceding property.

7. Now create a file called `CommentAuthor.php` in the same directory containing the `CommentAuthor` entity class as shown in the following code:

```php
<?php

namespace Blog\Entity;

use Doctrine\ORM\Mapping\Entity;

/**
 * Comment author entity
 *
 * @Entity
 */
class CommentAuthor extends Author
{
    /**
     * @var Comment[]
     *
     * @OneToMany(targetEntity="Comment",
mappedBy="commentAuthor")
     */
    protected $comments;
}
```

This entity class is very similar to the `PostAuthor` class, except that its association is related to `Comment` instead of `Post`, and it doesn't have a `bio` property.

Another table called `CommentAuthor` will be created in the database. This table will be completely independent of the `PostAuthor` table.

8. Write the getter and setter for the same property after adding the preceding code.

9. We also need to add the owning-side of the association. Open the `src/Blog/Entity/Comment.php` file and add the following properties:

```php
/**
 * @var CommentAuthor
 *
 * @ManyToOne(targetEntity="CommentAuthor",
 *   inversedBy="comments")
 */
protected $author;
```

10. After you've completed the previous step, add the getter and setter.

11. To understand how this type of inheritance is handled by Doctrine, and to test our code, we will create a fixture by inserting sample data in the `src/DataFixtures/LoadAuthorData.php` file as shown by the following code:

```php
<?php

namespace Blog\DataFixtures;

use Blog\Entity\Comment;
use Blog\Entity\CommentAuthor;
use Blog\Entity\Post;
use Blog\Entity\PostAuthor;
use Doctrine\Common\DataFixtures\Doctrine;
use Doctrine\Common\DataFixtures\FixtureInterface;
use Doctrine\Common\Persistence\ObjectManager;

/**
 * Author fixtures
 */
class LoadAuthorData implements FixtureInterface
{
    /**
     * {@inheritDoc}
     */
    public function load(ObjectManager $manager)
    {
        $postAuthor = new PostAuthor();
        $postAuthor->setName('George Abitbol');
        $postAuthor->setEmail('gabitbol@example.com');
        $postAuthor->setBio('L\'homme le plus classe du monde');

        $manager->persist($postAuthor);

        $post = new Post();
        $post->setTitle('My post');
        $post->setBody('Lorem ipsum');
        $post->setPublicationDate(new \DateTime());
        $post->setauthor($postAuthor);

        $manager->persist($post);

        $commentAuthor = new CommentAuthor();
        $commentAuthor->setName('Kévin Dunglas');
```

```
$commentAuthor->setEmail('dunglas@gmail.com');

$manager->persist($commentAuthor);

$comment = new Comment();
$comment->setBody('My comment');
$comment->setAuthor($commentAuthor);
$comment->setPublicationDate(new \DateTime());

$post->addComment($comment);
$manager->persist($comment);

$manager->flush();
    }
}
```

This fixture creates instances of `Post`, `PostAuthor`, `Comment`, and `CommentAuthor` and then persists them to the database.

12. Update the following schema:

    ```
    php vendor/bin/doctrine orm:schema-tool:update --force
    ```

    The following ER diagram represents the schema that will be generated on using MySQL as DBMS:

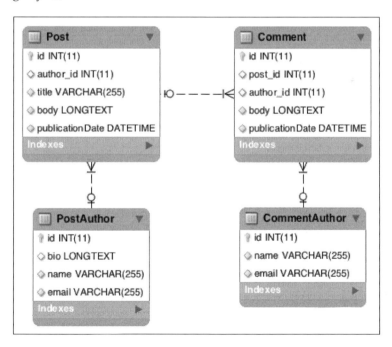

Even if the `PostAuthor` and `CommentAuthor` classes both inherit from the `Author` Mapped Superclass, their corresponding SQL schemas do not share anything and are not related.

13. Then load the fixtures with the following command:

    ```
    php bin/load-fixtures.php
    ```

14. Use the SQLite client to show the inserted content in each table with the following command:

    ```
    sqlite3 data/blog.db "SELECT * FROM PostAuthor; SELECT *
        FROM CommentAuthor;"
    ```

    After the preceding steps George's and my details should appear as follows:

    1 | L'homme le plus classe du monde | George Abitbol | gabitbol@example. com

    1 | Kévin Dunglas | dunglas@gmail.com

 For practice, the UI of the author feature is used. An example is provided in the bonus code sample available on the Packt website.

Using Single Table Inheritance

With Single Table Inheritance, data of all the classes of the hierarchy will be stored in the same database table. A column for every property of every child class will be created.

This mapping strategy suits very well for a simple type of hierarchy and performs well while querying both the same and different types of entities.

To change from Mapped Super Class to Single Table Inheritance, we will just make some modifications to the classes we just created:

1. Open the `src/Blog/Entity/Author.php` file and find the following snippet:

    ```
    use Doctrine\ORM\Mapping\MappedSuperclass;
    use Doctrine\ORM\Mapping\Id;
    use Doctrine\ORM\Mapping\GeneratedValue;
    use Doctrine\ORM\Mapping\Column;

    /**
    * Author mapped superclass
    *
    * @MappedSuperclass
    ```

2. Replace the preceding snippet with the following snippet:

```
use Doctrine\ORM\Mapping\Entity;
use Doctrine\ORM\Mapping\InheritanceType;
use Doctrine\ORM\Mapping\Id;
use Doctrine\ORM\Mapping\GeneratedValue;
use Doctrine\ORM\Mapping\Column;

/**
 * Author superclass
 *
 * @Entity
 * @InheritanceType("SINGLE_TABLE")
```

3. Update the schema and load the fixtures again with the following queries:

```
php vendor/bin/doctrine orm:schema-tool:update --force
php bin/load-fixtures.php
```

The following screenshot is the ER diagram for the Single Table Inheritance type:

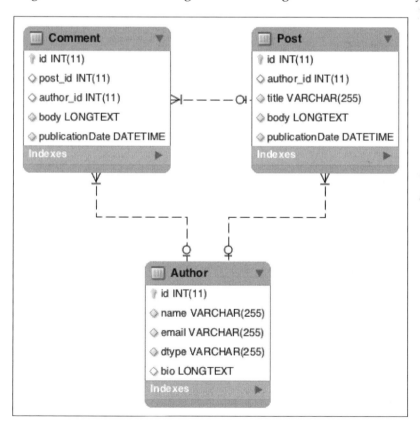

Data of both `PostAuthor` and `CommentAuthor` entities is now persisted in a unique database table called `Author`.

The entity type is identified in the table, thanks to a **discriminator column** added, and automatically managed, by Doctrine.

By default, this discriminator column is called `dtype` and the Doctrine type `string`. These values can be overridden thanks to the `@DiscriminatorColumn` annotation. This annotation should be used on the entity class marked with the `@InheritanceType` annotation (here, the `Author` class).

The value stored in this column is used by Doctrine to determine the type of entity class to hydrate for a given database row. It defaults to the name of the entity class (not fully qualified) in lowercase. The used value for each entity class can also be overridden by adding an annotation on the parent entity class: `@DiscriminatorMap`.

All these annotations and the Single Table Inheritance type are documented at:

```
http://docs.doctrine-project.org/en/latest/reference/inheritance-
mapping.html#single-table-inheritance
```

To look at the data we have inserted in the `Author` table with our fixtures, run the following command:

```
sqlite3 data/blog.db "SELECT * FROM Author"
```

The result should be as follows:

1 | Kévin Dunglas | dunglas@gmail.com | commentauthor |

2 | George Abitbol | gabitbol@example.com | postauthor | L'homme le plus classe du monde

Using Class Table Inheritance

The last strategy provided by Doctrine is the Class Table Inheritance. Data of each class of the hierarchy is stored in a specific database table. All the tables of the hierarchy are joined during the data retrieval time.

Because of the massive use of joins, this strategy is less efficient than Single Table Inheritance, especially with Big Data. The more descendant classes you add, the more joins are needed to retrieve data, and the slower the querying.

But because every entity class of the hierarchy is mapped to its own table, this strategy also allows great flexibility. Creating or modifying an entity class only affects its directly related database table. In cases where performance is not a priority and the data model is complex, this type of inheritance can be a solution to limit or avoid complex, and even risky, migrations.

As for Single Table Inheritance, we just need to make minor changes to create our `Author` data model using Class Table Inheritance with the following steps:

1. Open the `src/Blog/Entity/Author.php` file and find the following `@InheritanceType` annotation we added to use Single Table Inheritance:

    ```
    * @InheritanceType("SINGLE_TABLE")
    ```

2. Replace the argument `SINGLE_TABLE` by the following argument:

    ```
    * @InheritanceType("JOINED")
    ```

3. Update the schema and load the fixtures, again with the following query:

    ```
    php vendor/bin/doctrine orm:schema-tool:update --force
    php bin/load-fixtures.php
    ```

    The following ER diagram represents the generated schema, again using MySQL:

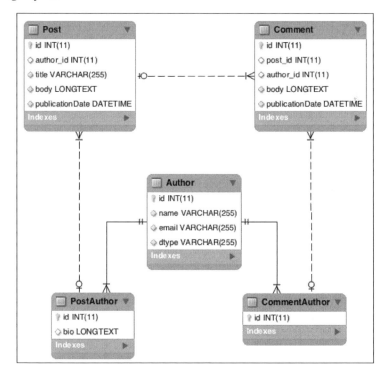

The Author table contains shared data between PostAuthor and CommentAuthor entity classes. These child classes only hold their specific data. Their id columns are foreign keys referencing the id column of the Author table. This allows data linking because the ID in a table storing data of descendant classes is the same as the ID in the table storing data of the top class.

As for Single Table Inheritance, a discriminator column allows Doctrine to identify the entity class corresponding to the database table's rows. Their default names and values are the same. They can also be overridden through @DicriminatorColumn and @DicriminatorMap annotations on the topmost entity class of the hierarchy (here, Author).

 Class Table Inheritance allows referencing the topmost class of a hierarchy in associations, but the loading feature will not work anymore.

For further information about Class Table Inheritance, refer to the documentation available at http://docs.doctrine-project.org/en/latest/reference/inheritance-mapping.html#class-table-inheritance.

4. To show data we have inserted with fixtures in the Author, CommentAuthor and PostAuthor tables, run the following query with the SQLite client:

```
sqlite3 data/blog.db "SELECT * FROM Author; SELECT * FROM
    PostAuthor; SELECT * FROM CommentAuthor;"
```

The following is the expected result:

1 | Kévin Dunglas | dunglas@gmail.com | commentauthor

2 | George Abitbol | gabitbol@example.com | postauthor

2 | L'homme le plus classe du monde

1

Getting started with events

The Doctrine Common component comes with a built-in event system. It allows dispatching and subscribing to custom events, but its main purpose is to manage entity-related events.

In *Chapter 1, Getting Started with Doctrine 2*, we learned about entity managers, entity states, and Unit Of Work. Entity Managers (and their underlying UnitOfWork objects) dispatch events when the state of the entity changes and when data is stored, updated, and removed from the database. They are called lifecycle events.

 Doctrine also emits some events not directly related to the entity lifecycle.

Doctrine ORM provides the following bunch of lifecycle events:

- preRemove: This event occurs when the state of the entity is set to removed

- postRemove: This event occurs after the removal of an entity's data from the database

- prePersist: This event occurs when the state of the entity passes from new to managed

- postPersist: This event occurs after the INSERT SQL query has been executed

- preUpdate: This event occurs before the UPDATE SQL query

- postUpdate: This event occurs after the UPDATE SQL query

- postLoad: This event occurs after the load or the refresh of the entity in the EntityManager

 The full documentation of events (including the non-lifecycle one) on Doctrine ORM is available in the online documentation at http://docs.doctrine-project.org/en/latest/reference/events.html.

Lifecycle callbacks

Lifecycle callbacks are the easiest way to use these events. They allow executing methods directly defined in entity classes when the lifecycle event occurs.

In our blog, we store the date of the publication of posts and comments. Thanks to lifecycle callbacks and to the prePersist event, it's possible to automatically set this date the first time an entity is passed through the persist() method of its Entity Manager (when the state goes from new to managed):

1. Open the Post.php file in the src/Blog/Entity/ folder and the Comment.php file in the src/Blog/Entity/ folder.

2. Add the following use statements to both the files:

```
use Doctrine\ORM\Mapping\HasLifecycleCallbacks;
use Doctrine\ORM\Mapping\PrePersist;
```

3. Add the `@HasLifecycleCallbacks` annotations next to `@Entity` to both the files. This enables lifecycle callbacks in these two entity classes.

4. Then, add the following method to both the files, setting the publication date when the `prePersist` event occurs:

```
/**
 * Sets publication date to now at persist time
 *
 * @PrePersist
 */
public function setPublicationDateOnPrePersist()
{
    if (!$this->publicationDate) {
        $this->publicationDate = new \DateTime();
    }
}
```

This method is executed when a `Comment` or `Post` entity is passed through the `persist()` method of an entity manager. It sets the `publicationDate` property to the current time if it has not been already done.

These callback methods can take an optional argument, allowing access to the `EntityManager` and `UnitOfWork` (giving access to the underlying changeset) objects related to the entity which can be referenced at:

```
http://docs.doctrine-project.org/en/latest/
reference/events.html#lifecycle-callbacks-event-
argument
```

Thanks to this tweak, we can remove calls using `setPublicationDate()` methods in `web/view-post.php` and `web/edit-post.php`.

A popular library you should try is *Gediminas Morkevičius* `DoctrineExtensions`. It contains many useful behaviors for Doctrine, including, but not limited to, timestamps, translations, soft delete, and nested sets. The Doctrine extensions can be found at:

```
https://github.com/l3pp4rd/DoctrineExtensions
```

Knowing about event listeners and event subscribers

Doctrine provides more powerful ways to deal with events: **event subscribers** and **event listeners**. Unlike lifecycle callbacks that are defined directly in entity classes, both must be defined in external classes. We will take a quick look at them.

The main difference between listeners and subscribers is that listeners are attached to an event, and subscribers register themselves to events.

Let's create a listener that will strip some French insults from published comments in the `src/Blog/Event/InsultEventListener.php` file:

```php
<?php

namespace Blog\Event;

use Blog\Entity\Comment;
use Doctrine\Common\Persistence\Event\LifecycleEventArgs;

/**
 * Censors French insults in comments
 */
class InsultEventListener
{
    /**
     * Censors on the prePersist event
     *
     * @param LifecycleEventArgs $args
     */
    public function prePersist(LifecycleEventArgs $args)
    {
        $entity = $args->getObject();

        if ($entity instanceof Comment) {
            // Use a black list instead, or better don't do that,
            it's useless
            $entity->setBody(str_ireplace(['connard',
                'lenancker'], 'censored', $entity->getBody()));
        }
    }
}
```

And now, we will create an event subscriber that will send an e-mail
to a post author when a comment is posted in the `src/Blog/Event/`
`MailAuthorOnCommentEventSubscriber.php` file, as shown in the following code:

```php
<?php

namespace Blog\Event;

use Doctrine\Common\EventSubscriber;
use Doctrine\ORM\Event\LifecycleEventArgs;
use Doctrine\ORM\Events;
use Blog\Entity\Comment;

/**
 * Mails a post author when a new comment is published
 */
class MailAuthorOnCommentEventSubscriber implements EventSubscriber
{

    /**
     * {@inheritDoc}
     */
    public function getSubscribedEvents()
    {
        return [Events::postPersist];
    }

    /**
     * Mails the Post's author when a new Comment is published
     *
     * @param LifecycleEventArgs $args
     */
    public function postPersist(LifecycleEventArgs $args)
    {
        $entity = $args->getObject();

        if ($entity instanceof Comment) {
            if ($entity->getPost()->getAuthor() && $entity-
                >getAuthor()) {
                mail(
                    $entity->getPost()->getAuthor()->getEmail(),
                      'New comment!',
                    sprintf('%s published a new comment on your
                      post %s', $entity->getAuthor()->getName(),
                        $entity->getPost()->getTitle())
```

```
                );
            }
        }

    }
}
```

Events' listener and subscriber methods' names must match the name of the events they want to catch. The entity related to the event and it's entity manager are available through the `$args` parameter. In our examples, we only used the entity.

Events' listeners and subscribers are only called when the event they have subscribed to is dispatched, whatever the type of entity. It's their responsibility to filter entities by type. This is why we use the `instanceof` keyword to check whether entities are of the type `Comment`.

Unlike event listeners, event subscribers must implement the `EventSubscriber` interface. The `getSubscribedEvents()` method must return an array of events to listen to.

The last step is to register these events' listeners and subscribers through an Event Manager. Unlike for lifecycle callbacks, this is not handled automatically.

Open the `src/bootstrap.php` file and add the following use statements:

```php
use Doctrine\ORM\Events;
use Doctrine\Common\EventManager;
use Blog\Event\InsultEventListener;
use Blog\Event\MailAuthorOnCommentEventSubscriber;
```

Then find the following line of code:

```php
$entityManager = EntityManager::create($dbParams, $config,
    $eventManager);
```

Replace the preceding line with the following code snippet:

```php
$eventManager = new EventManager();
$eventManager->addEventListener([Events::prePersist], new
    InsultEventListener());
$eventManager->addEventSubscriber(new
    MailAuthorOnCommentEventSubscriber());

$entityManager = EntityManager::create($dbParams, $config,
    $eventManager);
```

We instantiate an Event Manager, and we register our listener and our subscriber. For the listener, we need to tell for which events it should be called. The subscriber registers itself to events it is interested in.

The Event Manager object must be linked to the entity manager when it is created; this is why it is passed as the third argument of the `EntityManager::create()` static method (see *Chapter 1, Getting Started with Doctrine 2*).

Writing native queries

In the previous chapter, we learned how to create DQL queries through the `QueryBuilder`. But DQL has some limitations (that is, queries cannot contain subqueries in FROM and JOIN clauses), and sometimes you want to use specific features of your DBMS (that is, MySQL full-text search). In such cases you need to write native SQL queries.

The NativeQuery class

The `NativeQuery` class allows you to execute native SQL queries and to get their results as Doctrine entities. Only SELECT queries are supported.

To experiment with this feature, we will create a new command that displays the 100 most recent comments. This can be useful to moderate them.

Create a file containing this new command called `last-comments.php` in the `bin/` directory of the app.

```php
<?php

require_once __DIR__.'/../src/bootstrap.php';

use Doctrine\ORM\Query\ResultSetMappingBuilder;

const NUMBER_OF_RESULTS = 100;

  $resultSetMappingBuilder = new
    ResultSetMappingBuilder($entityManager);
  $resultSetMappingBuilder-
    >addRootEntityFromClassMetadata('Blog\Entity\Comment', 'c');
  $resultSetMappingBuilder->addJoinedEntityFromClassMetadata(
    'Blog\Entity\Post',
    'p',
    'c',
    'post',
    [
```

```
            'id' => 'post_id',
            'body' => 'post_body',
            'publicationDate' => 'post_publication_date',
            'author_id' => 'post_author_id'
    ])
    ;


$sql = <<<SQL
SELECT id, publicationDate, body, post_id
FROM Comment
ORDER BY publicationDate DESC
LIMIT :limit
SQL;


$query = $entityManager->createNativeQuery($sql,
    $resultSetMappingBuilder);
$query->setParameter('limit', NUMBER_OF_RESULTS);
$comments = $query->getResult();

foreach ($comments as $comment) {
    echo sprintf('Comment #%s%s', $comment->getId(), PHP_EOL);
    echo sprintf('Post #%s%s', $comment->getPost()->getId(),
        PHP_EOL);
    echo sprintf('Date of publication: %s%s', $comment-
        >getPublicationDate()->format('r'), PHP_EOL);
    echo sprintf('Body: %s%s', $comment->getBody(), PHP_EOL);
    echo PHP_EOL;
}
```

The `ResultSetMappingBuilder` class is designed to map SQL query results to Doctrine entities. The call to its `addRootEntityFromClassMetadata()` method specifies the main entity class that will be hydrated (first parameter) as well as its internal alias (second parameter). Here it is `Comment`.

The `addJoinedEntityFromClassMetadata()` method permits you to populate an association of the root entity. The first parameter is the entity class. The second is the internal alias of this entity. The third is the internal alias of its parent entity. The fourth is the name of the relation in its parent entity class. And the last is an array of mappings between an entity's properties and SQL query aliases.

This last parameter is useful when SQL column names don't match entity's property names. Here, we use it to populate the `id` property of the related post with the `post_id` column of the `Comment` table.

Both `Comment` and `Post` database tables have columns called `body`, `publication_date`, and `author_id`. To get around this conflict, we map the `Post` entity properties respectively to `post_body`, `post_publication_date`, and `post_author_id` columns. You noticed that the SQL query doesn't return these columns. This is not a problem; they will be ignored.

The `createNativeQuery()` method of the `EntityManager` takes the SQL query and the `ResultSetMappingBuilder` as parameters. Like DQL queries, SQL queries can use named parameters. They will automatically escape to prevent SQL injection attacks.

Thanks to `NativeQuery` and `ResultSetMappingBuilder` classes, the result of the query is a collection of `Comment` entities (partially hydrated) with their related `Post` entity (having only the `id` property hydrated).

Run the following code to see the last 100 comments:

```
php bin/list-comments.php
```

Doctrine DBAL

Doctrine provides an even lower level way to issue native SQL queries. You can retrieve the underlying DBAL connection through the `EntityManager` and use it directly.

This is useful to execute native `UPDATE` and `DELETE` queries and to retrieve data that is not intended to populate entities. Of course, do that only if you have a good reason or use DQL's `SELECT`, `UPDATE`, or `DELETE` queries instead.

To illustrate native queries through DBAL, we will create another command that displays some simple stats about our blog.

 As they don't use any DBMS-specific query, this command should be executed through ORM. Native queries are used here only to illustrate this feature.

Create a file for this new command called `stats.php` in the `bin/` directory with the following code:

```php
<?php

require_once __DIR__.'/../src/bootstrap.php';

$sql = <<<SQL
SELECT
  COUNT(id) AS nb,
  MAX(publicationDate) AS latest
FROM Post
UNION
SELECT
  COUNT(id),
  MAX(publicationDate)
FROM Comment
SQL;

$query = $entityManager->getConnection()->query($sql);
$result = $query->fetchAll();

  echo sprintf('Number of posts: %d%s', $result[0]['nb'],
    PHP_EOL);
  echo sprintf('Last post: %s%s', $result[0]['latest'], PHP_EOL);
  echo sprintf('Number of comments: %d%s', $result[1]['nb'],
    PHP_EOL);
  echo sprintf('Last comment: %s%s', $result[1]['latest'],
    PHP_EOL);
```

We use the `EntityManager` to retrieve the underlying `Doctrine\DBAL\Connection` with the `getConnection()` method. DBAL's `Connection` is just a thin wrapper around `PDO` and its API is very similar. We use it to compute the total number and the last publication date of posts and comments.

To show them, run the following command:

```
php bin/stats.php
```

Summary

The last chapter was a quick overview of some advanced features of Doctrine: handling Inheritance though Mapped Superclass, Single Table Inheritance, and Class Table Inheritance; the Doctrine event system including lifecycle callbacks, listeners, and subscribers; and finally how to unleash the power of the underlying DBMS for specific use cases with native queries.

Throughout this book, we have learned how to use the Doctrine ORM to create a stable model layer in our PHP applications. We are now familiar with concepts behind Doctrine components and we are able to smartly use its ORM. We also looked at the most powerful (but also complex) features, including entity managers and entity states, mapping information, associations, DQL, hydration, inheritance, events, and native queries. There is still a lot to learn, and many of these topics deserve a dedicated book of their own.

Again, the online documentation of the Doctrine project (available at `http://www.doctrine-project.org/`) is comprehensive and full of advanced examples.

Recall for the last time that to use Doctrine efficiently in production, a cache system (APC, Memcache, and Reddis), depending on your needs and of what is available on your server platform, must be used.

One last thing, Doctrine is free and open source software welcoming your contributions: bug reports and fixes, documentation, and adding new features.

Index

Symbols

@Column annotation 23-25
@DiscriminatorColumn annotation 84
@DiscriminatorMap annotation 84
@Entity annotation 22
@GeneratedValue annotation 24
@Id annotation 24
@Index annotation 22
@InheritanceType annotation 84
@JoinColumn annotation 40
@JoinTable annotation 40
@ManyToMany annotation, with tags 52
@ManyToOne annotation, with comment system 40
@OneToMany annotation, with comment system 40
@Table annotation 22
@UniqueConstraint annotation 23

A

addComment() method 44
addJoinedEntityFromClassMetadata() method 93
addRootEntityFromClassMetadata() method 93
app
  bootstrapping 13, 14
  folder structure 10
association types, Doctrine
  Many-To-Many 39
  Many-To-One 39
  One-To-One 39

B

Behat
  URL 28
bidirectional association 40

C

CASCADE operations 55
Class Table Inheritance
  about 84
  using 84-86
command line tools, Doctrine
  configuring 16, 17
Comment entity class
  creating 41, 42
  properties 41
comments
  about 40
  counting 71-73
  creating 47-51
  fixtures, adding for 46, 47
  listing 47-51
comment system
  Comment entity class, creating 41, 42
  comments, creating 47-51
  comments, listing 47-51
  database schema, updating 45
  fixtures, adding for comments 46, 47
  index, updating 51
  inverse side, adding to Post entity class 43, 44
Common 5
Composer
  about 10

installing 11
composer.json file 12
createNativeQuery() method 94
createQueryBuilder() method 66
CSRF
　URL 31
curl
　about 7
　URL 7
custom entity repositories
　about 64
　creating 64, 65

D

Database Abstraction Layer. *See* **DBAL**
database schema
　creating 26, 27
Data Fixtures
　about 28
　installing 28, 29
Data Mapper 8
DBAL 5, 62, 94, 95
DELETE CASCADE operations 55
Dependency Injection pattern
　URL 16
detach() method 9
discriminator column 84
DocBlocks 20
Doctrine
　association types 39, 40
　Entity Manager, using 14, 16
　installing 11-13
　learning 6
　mapping types 25
　prerequisites 7
　URL, for documentation 7, 23
Doctrine annotations
　@Column annotation 23, 24
　@Entity annotation 22
　@GeneratedValue annotation 24
　@Id annotation 24
　@Index annotation 22
　@Table annotation 22
　@UniqueConstraint annotation 23
　mapping with 22
Doctrine ORM
　URL, for documentation 87

Doctrine project 5
Doctrine Query Language. *See* **DQL**
domain-specific languages
　about 61
　URL 61
DQL 61
DQL query
　running 62

E

Entity Manager
　about 8
　using 14, 16
EntityManager class 40
entity repositories
　about 9, 63
　using 63, 64
event listeners 89, 91
events
　about 86
　lifecycle callbacks 87, 88
event subscribers
　about 89
　creating 90, 91

F

find() method 9, 63
findWithCommentCount() method 72
findWithComments() method 66, 68
fixtures
　about 28
　adding, for comments 46, 47
flush() method 8, 9, 29

G

getOneOrNullResult() method 68
getters
　generating 21

H

Hibernate
　about 61
　URL 61
HQL 61

I

inheritance
  implementing 75
inheritance implementation
  Class Table Inheritance, using 78-86
  Mapped Superclasses, using 76, 77
  Single Table Inheritance, using 82-84
installation, Composer 11
installation, Data Fixtures 28-30
installation, Doctrine 11-13
install command 13
inverse side
  adding, to Post entity class 43, 44

L

lifecycle callbacks 87, 88
lifecycle events, Doctrine ORM
  postLoad 87
  postPersist 87
  postRemove 87
  postUpdate 87
  prePersist 87
  preRemove 87
  preUpdate 87
LoadPostData class 29

M

Many-To-Many association 39
Many-To-One association 39
Mapped Superclasses
  about 76
  using 76-82
mapping types, Doctrine 25

N

native queries
  DBAL 94, 95
  NativeQuery class 92, 93
  writing 92
NativeQuery class 92, 93

O

Object Document Mappers (ODM) 7

Object Relational Mapper (ORM) 5, 55
One-To-One association 39

P

Packagist 12
PDO 5
persist() method 9
PHP CLI
  URL 7
PHP Data Objects
  URL 5
phpDocumentator 20
PHP Specification Request
  URL 12
Post entity class
  about 19
  creating 20
  inverse side, adding to 43, 44
  properties 20
  updating 54-56
postLoad event 87
postPersist event 87
postRemove event 87
posts
  creating 33
  deleting 37
  editing 33
  listing 31, 33
  tags, managing of 58, 59
postUpdate event 87
prePersist event 87
preRemove event 87
preUpdate event 87

Q

QueryBuilder
  about 65
  starting 66-68

R

removeComment() method 44
remove() method 10
REST
  URL 31

S

separation of concerns
  URL 31
setters
  generating 21
Single Table Inheritance
  about 82
  using 82-84
SQLite
  URL 7
Symfony 69
Symfony Validator Component
  URL 24

T

Tag entity class
  creating, steps 52-54
  properties 52
tag filtering 69

tag fixtures
  creating 56, 57
tags
  about 52
  managing, of posts 58, 59
  Post entity class, updating 54-56
  schema, updating 56
  Tag entity class, creating 52, 53
  tag fixtures, creating 56, 57
  used, for filtering posts 69, 70

U

unidirectional association 40
Unit of Work design pattern 8
user interface
  creating 30
  page creation, for creating posts 33, 36, 37
  page creation, for deleting posts 37
  page creation, for editing posts 33, 36, 37
  page creation, for listing posts 31, 33

Thank you for buying
Persistence in PHP with Doctrine ORM

About Packt Publishing

Packt, pronounced 'packed', published its first book "*Mastering phpMyAdmin for Effective MySQL Management*" in April 2004 and subsequently continued to specialize in publishing highly focused books on specific technologies and solutions.

Our books and publications share the experiences of your fellow IT professionals in adapting and customizing today's systems, applications, and frameworks. Our solution based books give you the knowledge and power to customize the software and technologies you're using to get the job done. Packt books are more specific and less general than the IT books you have seen in the past. Our unique business model allows us to bring you more focused information, giving you more of what you need to know, and less of what you don't.

Packt is a modern, yet unique publishing company, which focuses on producing quality, cutting-edge books for communities of developers, administrators, and newbies alike. For more information, please visit our website: www.packtpub.com.

About Packt Open Source

In 2010, Packt launched two new brands, Packt Open Source and Packt Enterprise, in order to continue its focus on specialization. This book is part of the Packt Open Source brand, home to books published on software built around Open Source licences, and offering information to anybody from advanced developers to budding web designers. The Open Source brand also runs Packt's Open Source Royalty Scheme, by which Packt gives a royalty to each Open Source project about whose software a book is sold.

Writing for Packt

We welcome all inquiries from people who are interested in authoring. Book proposals should be sent to author@packtpub.com. If your book idea is still at an early stage and you would like to discuss it first before writing a formal book proposal, contact us; one of our commissioning editors will get in touch with you.

We're not just looking for published authors; if you have strong technical skills but no writing experience, our experienced editors can help you develop a writing career, or simply get some additional reward for your expertise.

Learning FuelPHP for Effective PHP Development

ISBN: 978-1-78216-036-6   Paperback: 104 pages

Use the flexible FuelPHP framework to quickly and effectively create PHP applications

1. Scaffold with oil - the FuelPHP command-line tool

2. Build an administration quickly and effectively

3. Create your own project using FuelPHP

Instant PhpStorm Starter

ISBN: 978-1-84969-394-3   Paperback: 86 pages

Learn professional PHP development with PhpStorm

1. Learn something new in an Instant! A short, fast, focused guide delivering immediate results.

2. Learn PHPStorm from scratch, from downloading to installation with no prior knowledge required

3. Enter, modify, and inspect the source code with as much automation as possible

4. Simple, full of easy-to-follow procedures and intuitive illustrations, this book will set you speedily on the right track

Please check **www.PacktPub.com** for information on our titles

Symfony 1.3 Web Application Development

ISBN: 978-1-84719-456-5   Paperback: 228 pages

Design, develop, and deploy feature-rich, high-performance PHP web applications using the Symfony framework

1. Create powerful web applications by leveraging the power of this Model-View-Controller-based framework

2. Covers all the new features of version 1.3 – many exciting plug-ins for you

3. Learn by doing without getting into too much theoretical detail – create a "real-life" milkshake store application

Expert PHP 5 Tools

ISBN: 978-1-84719-838-9   Paperback: 468 pages

Proven enterprise development tools and best practices for designing, coding, testing, and deploying PHP applications

1. Best practices for designing, coding, testing, and deploying PHP applications – all the information in one book

2. Learn to write unit tests and practice test-driven development from an expert

3. Set up a professional development environment with integrated debugging capabilities

4. Develop your own coding standard and enforce it automatically

Please check **www.PacktPub.com** for information on our titles

3750393R00068

Printed in Germany
by Amazon Distribution
GmbH, Leipzig